D0947311

THE THEATRE OF
JEAN ANOUILH

Jean Anouilh *Study by Baron (Copyright Camera Press Ltd)*

H. G. MCINTYRE PH.D.
Lecturer in French University of Strathclyde

THE THEATRE OF JEAN ANOUILH

BARNES & NOBLE BOOKS
TOTOWA, NEW JERSEY

First published in the USA 1981 *by*
Barnes & Noble Books
81 Adams Drive
Totowa, New Jersey, 07512

ISBN: 0–389–20182–0

Phototypeset by Input Typesetting Ltd, London SW19 8DR
and printed in Great Britain by Mackays of Chatham Ltd

Contents

	Page
Abbreviations	6
Introduction	7
1 First Plays	14
2 The Play as Game	24
3 Tragedy and Myth	42
4 *L'Invitation au château*	59
5 The Farce of Life	68
6 Heroes and Antiheroes	85
7 *La Grotte*	102
8 The Play as Pretext	112
Conclusion	128
Appendix	140
Bibliography	157
Index	163

Abbreviations

The following abbreviations, completed by page numbers, are used immediately after a quotation in the body of the text and in the footnotes. Page numbers refer to the standard *La Table Ronde* edition of the collected plays.

PN: *Pièces noires*
NPN: *Nouvelles pièces noires*
PR: *Pièces roses*
PB: *Pièces brillantes*
PG: *Pièces grinçantes*
NPG: *Nouvelles pièces grinçantes*
PC: *Pièces costumées*
PBQ: *Pièces baroques*
PS: *Pièces secrètes*

Longer titles are normally given in shortened form in the text—*e.g. L'Hurluberlu . . .*, *Le Boulanger . . .*, *Tu étais si gentil . . .* The full titles will be found in the chronology of Anouilh's professional life in the Appendix.

Acknowledgments

We are indebted to the Éditions de la Table Ronde for permission to print quotations from Anouilh's works, and to the University of California Press for permission to reproduce some short extracts from Leonard C. Pronko: *The World of Jean Anouilh* (Copyright © 1961 by the Regents of the University of California Press).

Introduction

Jean Anouilh is one of France's most popular and successful playwrights. His career in the theatre has spanned fifty years and almost as many plays. He has also written for the cinema and television and, in more recent years, has won praise as a producer, both of his own work and that of other dramatists. Anouilh's reputation is, indeed, international. His plays are translated into several languages and have been staged in places as far apart as London and New York, Hamburg and Rio de Janeiro. Along with his success he has earned admiration for his command of stagecraft. Many would regard him as the most gifted craftsman of his generation and even his critics acknowledge his seemingly effortless mastery of dramatic technique.

Too much success, however, can be a drawback, as Anouilh has discovered:

Voilà pas mal de temps que je m'occupe de théâtre et avec assez de bonheur pour que cela ait paru louche à certains . . .[1]

In intellectual and academic circles, in particular, Anouilh is often viewed with suspicion and disdain. His very popularity and talent are held against him. Having acquired a taste for success, it is felt, he has allowed his technical facility in the theatre to replace real intellectual depth. A summary of his career by the French writer and critic Pierre-Henri Simon is well worth quoting at some length. It is a model of its kind, incorporating many of the criticisms of Anouilh which have become standard:

Il est arrivé à Jean Anouilh l'accident qui guette les écrivains trop habiles: vient un moment où la perfection du métier nuit à la densité du sens. L'invention des effets recouvre la force de l'émotion créatrice, le brio du style finit par jouer dans un automatisme gratuit qui échappe à la pression de l'idée. Ayant dit l'essentiel dans les œuvres de jeunesse et de la première maturité, un auteur plein de ruses et accoutumé aux aplaudissements dévie de ses intentions profondes pour s'attacher à des intérêts de cir-

[1] *Opéra*, March 7th, 1951.

constances, parfois des circonstances politiques, pour faire jaillir le rire de la satire ou de l'allusion.[1]

There are other writers, as popular and as talented as Anouilh, who do not draw down such criticisms upon their heads; but clearly Anouilh's career has been a disappointment for many. He is seen as a promising young dramatist of the thirties who achieved precocious maturity in *La Sauvage* (1934) and *Le Voyageur sans bagage* (1936), electrified audiences during the Occupation with his masterpiece *Antigone* (1942) and, some time after the war, began an uneven descent, with occasional highlights, to where he is now. The resulting conclusion is that his work as a whole is not considered worthy of serious study beside that of his more important contemporaries. His epitaph has already been written: "a gifted stylist with a shallow point of view."[2]

One can suggest several reasons for this state of affairs. Anouilh's very longevity in the theatre must make him seem outdated beside those 'younger' playwrights, Sartre, Ionesco or Beckett for example, who made their mark in the fifties and sixties, carried along on the floods of Existentialism and the Absurd. While they were providing the "intellectual events"[3] of those years, Anouilh seemed unable or unwilling to outgrow his own recurrent preoccupations and more traditional dramatic form. Having apparently nothing to contribute to new ideas and developments, he was gradually relegated well to the rear of that enterprising avant-garde which was forging the theatre of tomorrow. We can see a number of short-term prejudices at work here: the attraction of novelty, the trendy intellectualism of anything avant-garde or experimental and an accompanying suspicion of commercial success.

Anouilh himself, however, is also to blame. He has always refused to be identified with any one philosophy or school of thought and has always avoided or bluntly dismissed general comparisons between his work and other movements in literary history. On the contrary, he has deliberately chosen to emphasize, in his own words, that "I am not a serious man."[4] This attitude has been misunderstood and many have taken offence over the years at Anouilh's lack of seriousness, bad taste and penchant for old jokes and easy laughter. He has been accused of trivializing otherwise worthy subjects, Antigone, Joan of Arc and Thomas Becket for example, for want of

[1] P. H. Simon, *Théâtre et Destin*, p. 144.
[2] R. Brustein, *The Theatre of Revolt*, p. (viii).
[3] J. Harvey, *Anouilh*, p. (x).
[4] *New York Times*, Oct. 2nd 1960.

anything more constructive or penetrating to say. Indeed, he has dismayed even his admirers at times by declaring his modest ambition to be no more than an entertainer, providing work for actors and distracting audiences for a few hours from the worries of everyday life. Proud of his workmanship, he has adopted a "humble craftsman" pose which has become famous or infamous in its own right:

> I make plays as a chair-maker makes chairs. Chairs are made to be sat on and plays are made to be played, to provide actors with work and the public with entertainment.[1]

Many critics have taken Anouilh at his word and dismissed him as the popular entertainer he claims to be. There is, however, a more fundamental and serious bias behind this dismissal of Anouilh. It stems from the premium we place upon ideas in literature. All too often, especially when plays are read and not seen, the search for a play's ideas or philosophy replaces an appreciation of its true dramatic worth. There are types of openly propagandist theatre in which this hardly matters since the message is paramount and dramatic considerations secondary or incidental. In these cases it may well be enough to extract key speeches and discourse upon them. Rarely, if ever, will this do justice to Anouilh. He is not a propagandist for whom dramatic form is unimportant. On the contrary, we shall see that the dramatic form of his plays often embodies his deepest thoughts. We shall also see that those characters of his who seem to speak most authoritatively are in fact often caught in an ironic structure which must be grasped as a whole and against which their pronouncements must be measured.

This overall structure is frequently neglected and, in the search for ideas, Anouilh is found wanting because he does not seem to provide enough to sustain long and learned discussion after the curtain has fallen. H.D.F. Kitto takes up this prejudice in the introduction to his *Form and Meaning in Drama* and many of the observations he makes there are pertinent here. In particular, the self-reproach he addresses to his own earlier criticism might well be applied to much that has been written about Anouilh:

> It did not honestly or completely account for the form in which the dramatist had cast the play.[2]

It is an irksome and dispiriting business to read review after review in which critics dismiss months or years of creative effort

[1] *International Herald Tribune*, Oct. 18th 1970.
[2] H.D.F. Kitto, *Form and Meaning in Drama*, p. (v).

and assert their own superior judgment in the process. They condemn Anouilh for the obvious. This play is not a 'pure' or 'true' tragedy; that play revels in the worst excesses of melodrama and bad taste; yet another is a clumsy amalgam of time-worn and weary theatrical clichés. On this evidence they are quick to convict, without making a real effort to account for a play's form or apparent lack of it. It is not the least of contradictions in Anouilh criticism that, while his technical expertise is widely recognized, he is frequently condemned for his lapses. It is only reasonable to assume that Anouilh is well aware, long before his critics, that here he is borrowing a hackneyed device or there indulging in pastiche. The all important step, and the one that is not taken, is to ask conscientiously why.

The failure to do this has adversely affected Anouilh's critical reputation as a thinker in the theatre. It has limited his philosophy to the well-known themes which are used to characterize his work: the struggle to preserve a sense of personal purity in a degrading world, nostalgia for childhood innocence, the rejection of material happiness, the conflict between idealism and compromise, the influences of one's past and family background, the parent-child relationship. There is no doubt that these are Anouilh's most abiding preoccupations, some would say obsessions. But they overshadow a whole area of Anouilh's thought on aesthetic and theatrical matters which are just as characteristic and enduring as his famous themes. These have been neglected precisely because they are for the most part embodied or implicit in the dramatic form of his plays. Hence when critics are emphasizing the shortcomings of Anouilh's metaphysics, politics or social themes, they are often interpreting in other terms considerations which are primarily aesthetic in nature. In fact, Anouilh has much to say on the nature, practice and function of the theatre which is not expounded openly across the footlights: but then, the text is only one element in a medium which possesses a rich and powerful non-verbal language of its own. As Kitto remarks:

> There are several instances where the dramatist says things of the utmost importance without using a single word.[1]

Anouilh has shown a deep interest in the constituent elements, conventions, techniques and resources of his chosen medium. His long career as a working dramatist has brought him to grips with such fundamental questions as the relationship of character to plot,

[1] ibid.

the function of suspense, the construction and presentation of character, the effects of mixing different styles and genres, the relative merits of old theatrical conventions and modern innovations, the role of the audience in the theatre and the contribution they can make to the dramatic illusion.

By explaining these matters, we find another, very different Anouilh behind the mask of the "vieux boulevardier, honteux et pas franc"[1] which he wears. It is an Anouilh who, despite accusations of repetitiveness, lack of invention and complacency, has made a sustained effort over the years to adapt his own style to different values and a changing vision of the world. His relative conservatism in thought and technique is based on a coherent view of life and of the theatre's place in it and his reflections on his art are a pertinent contribution to modern thinking on the theatre. Moreover, despite his seeming complacency, we can see a clear ethical need, which grows throughout his work, to justify his privileged way of life by defining a function and value for the theatre in the world. Indeed, that constant debate between the artist, on the one hand, and his inspiration and materials on the other, which characterizes Anouilh's whole development is as much ethical as aesthetic in motivation.

Anouilh is a shy, modest and reticent man who dislikes the exhibitionism to which his profession is prone. He has not, like some of his contemporaries, produced as many theories as plays. It would be misleading, then, to portray him as a theorist of the drama. He would be the first to object. As a close friend and collaborator remarked:

Avec Jean Anouilh, jamais de théories sur le théâtre.[2]

Despite this, there does exist a considerable body of comment by Anouilh on the theatre which has not been as fully exploited as it might be.[3] One reason may be that it is scattered over many years and a variety of newspapers, periodicals and theatre programmes and is not easily accessible. It does, however, shed valuable light on his developing interests and convictions and will be used here wherever possible. This body of material qualifies somewhat Anouilh's reticence on such matters. The frequent insights it contains also enhance his standing as a thinker in and on the theatre.

It could justifiably be argued that emphasizing the technical side of Anouilh's preoccupations, in fact, shirks the real task of defending Anouilh as a thinker in more general terms; but Anouilh's

[1] Anouilh's self-description in P. Vandromme, *Jean Anouilh*, p. 231.
[2] J.D. Malclès in *Cahiers de la Compagnie Renaud-Barrault*, vol. 26, p. 41.
[3] Some of this material is reprinted in Vandromme, op. cit., pp. 139–244.

convictions on the practice of his art did not develop in a vacuum. Another of the several myths which have grown up around Anouilh is that, in his own phrase, "Je n'ai pas de biographie."[1] He is famous as a recluse, shunning publicity and, on occasion, slipping away early from his own first nights. He has fiercely defended his right to privacy outside the theatre. One can only respect this. Nonetheless, it is clear, from statements made by himself and by close friends and colleagues, that we can relate his maturation as an artist to various events in his life which have affected his outlook and left their mark upon his plays. To this end, the present study adopts a broadly chronological and evolutionary approach which divides his work into groups of plays, characterized by common concerns and corresponding to different periods of his life. No doubt, a future generation of critics will find more points of contact between life and work than Anouilh is prepared to admit to, but that study is for another time.

For the present time, this is a welcome advance in understanding Anouilh's development but it has a wider significance. It sets Anouilh's technical preoccupations in a human context and perspective. Through the very theatricality of life itself, as he sees it and recreates it on stage, Anouilh has much to say about the human predicament, about man as playwright, actor and spectator of his destiny, that has been neglected or distorted in the search for his ideas elsewhere. It is only in this wider context of the relationship of art to life that Anouilh's convictions on aesthetic matters assume their full value and importance. Seen in this wider context, they reveal that Anouilh has much to say on the function and value of art in life, the nature of self-consciousness, our perception of reality and man's relationship to his destiny which is worthy of consideration beside the philosophies of his more serious contemporaries.

Again, however, it must be emphasized that Anouilh's reflections result not in a theory but a play. We should approach them therefore in the spirit in which Henri Ghéon undertook to lecture on the same matters:

> Tout entier à mon art, j'ai réfléchi longuement sur mon art et je rassemble ici mes réflexions partiales.[2]

Anouilh's reflections are likewise those of a practising dramatist and equally partisan. They do not pretend to form a complete or rigorously coherent philosophy. On the other hand, they may well

[1] Anouilh's letter to H. Gignoux in 1946, reprinted in P. Ginestier, *Anouilh*, p. 225, and translated in L.C. Pronko, *The World of Jean Anouilh*, p. (xviii).
[2] H. Ghéon, *L'Art du théâtre*, p. 12.

offer “certaines choses que le critique (de profession) est peut-être moins bien placé pour savoir et voir.”[1]

[1] ibid.

I. First Plays

L'Hermine – Jézabel – La Sauvage

"Il n'est pas donné à tout le monde de pouvoir être heureux."
(Anouilh)

Anouilh's first plays are the work of a young man just out of his teens, living in the Paris of the early thirties on modest means, fascinated by the theatre and determined to make a career out of writing plays. They bear all the marks of his enthusiasm and determination. They are basically naturalistic dramas in which earnest young people face grave predicaments. The workmanship is conscientious, construction is tight and the tone serious, sometimes to the point of melodrama. These comments have now become commonplace about Anouilh's early work and they are certainly valid generalizations on the three plays of this chapter. These three constitute the core of Anouilh's serious output in the formative years from 1930 to 1934. It is worth remembering, however, they they represent less than half his actual output in this same short period. The other plays now exist in name only except an amusing curtain raiser, *Humulus le Muet*, and a full-length comedy, *Le Bal des Voleurs*, written in 1932.[1]

Obviously, then, there was already a comic vein in Anouilh's inspiration from the very outset. Indeed, with benefit of hindsight, Anouilh looks back on *Le Bal des Voleurs* in particular as the most significant of his early plays, in terms of his later development. But it was originally written in imitation of the successful Boulevard comedy of the day and intended for that lucrative market. No doubt even Anouilh at the time regarded it as a diversion from his more serious work. For this reason and for others which will become apparent later we shall leave consideration of it to the next chapter.

Even with the three plays that remain, however, the generalizations mentioned do a double disservice to Anouilh's early work. They emphasize the debt of these "pièces de type habituel"[2] to much of the well-made, serious drawing-room drama that preceded them in the nineteenth and early twentieth centuries and they create

[1] *Mandarine* (1929), which ran for 13 performances in 1933, and *Attile le Magnifique* (1930) and *Le petit Bonheur* (1935), which were never produced.
[2] P. Jolivet, *Le Théâtre de Jean Anouilh*, p. 19.

too uniform an impression of this short but formative period. They neglect therefore an evolution away from naturalism, seriousness and careful construction which is already discernible and reveals the presence of an individual temperament feeling its way towards its own distinctive and personal idiom. This significant development will be our main interest here since it prepares the way for an all-important change in Anouilh's attitude to the theatre which will take place in the next chapter and will influence the rest of his writing.

The first two plays, *L'Hermine* and *Jézabel*, demonstrate Anouilh's conscientious workmanship. They suggest a diffident young dramatist with more faith in the precision of his engineering than in the imagination or co-operation of his audience. He seems chiefly preoccupied with motivating his young heroes convincingly and this reduces the action to a linear progression. The first and second acts of *L'Hermine* offer the most relentless example of this. The hero, Frantz, is an orphan of modest origins who is in love with Monime, ward of his benefactor, the rich Duchesse de Granat. Desperate for money to give him the independence he needs to marry Monime, he has tried several unsuccessful business ventures. At the beginning of the play we find him asking Bentz, a rich financier, to help him stave off final bankruptcy. Denied by Bentz, what he regards as a last chance to win Monime by legitimate means, Frantz is driven closer and closer to murdering the Duchesse de Granat. The various steps in this macabre progression are introduced fairly obviously to this end. His friend, Philippe, a journalist, recounts the odd story of a young boy who, with the help of a pal, murdered his grandmother for the price of a trip to Paris. This story implants the idea of murder in Frantz's mind. He is goaded further along the road by his subsequent humiliating encounter with the overbearing old Duchesse, who reminds Frantz of his humble origins and ridicules his pretensions to marrying Monime. Then the hapless Marie-Anne, spinster companion to the Duchesse, tells her sad story of separation from a lifelong lover because of her financial dependence on her employer. The moral of this tale steels Frantz's resolve. Dramatic interest is maintained throughout by suspense: will Frantz murder the Duchesse? He does in the end by bludgeoning her to death with a hammer, but the brutality of the act and his apparent indifference afterwards horrify and alienate Monime. Seeing this, Frantz confesses to the police, whereupon Monime suddenly rediscovers her love for him. She throws herself at his feet as the final curtain falls. Despite the ambitious twist at the end, there is a good deal of truth in the impression that *L'Hermine* is "construite pour un acte et non sur une action".[1]

Jézabel is a slight advance on this. When the play begins its hero, Marc, also of poor background, has already forsaken his rich girl-friend, Jacqueline, for reasons as yet unknown. Again, however, the subsequent progress of the play amounts to an accumulative confirmation of his initial doubts. His mother, Jézabel, is an ageing nymphomaniac desperate for money to pay her latest lover's debts, so desperate in fact that she murders her husband with poisonous mushrooms to get at his savings. The vicious young maid, Georgette, uses her knowledge of this guilty secret to exert sexual blackmail on Marc who realizes he is not an entirely unwilling victim. Each discovery, first his mother's crime, then his own latent sensuality, inherited from her, widens the gulf between his background and Jacqueline's wealthy and happy family. When Jacqueline, whose love is greater than all obstacles, comes to reclaim Marc, he deliberately alienates her by pretending complicity in the murder, and then flees the stage.

There are only two years between this play and *La Sauvage* written in 1934, but *La Sauvage* is an immense leap forward in comparison. In it we find the same essential seriousness and direct appeal to our emotions. Thérèse Tarde, the heroine, is indeed a memorable and moving creation, the first in a line of such Anouilh heroines. Gone however is the linear progression of *L'Hermine* and *Jézabel*, in favour of a freer, more imaginative use of theatrical effects and a greater willingness to vary mood and rhythm by introducing comic episodes. Yet the basic situation is familiar. Thérèse is violinist in her father's small, third-rate café orchestra. She has, however, met and fallen in love with her Prince Charming in the person of Florent, a rich and famous virtuoso pianist. One evening she returns to the café where she works to find Florent, at her father's instigation, playing for a drunken customer. Suddenly she realizes for the first time the unbridgeable gap between their respective backgrounds. To the incomprehension of Florent and the despair of her parents, who see her forthcoming marriage as a lucrative affair, she rejects Florent and identifies almost hysterically with all the meanness and vulgarity of her parents and background. The first act ends inconclusively with Thérèse, her crisis over, sobbing in Florent's arms. It is the second act which breaks with the characteristic linearity of the two preceding plays. The curtain rises on Thérèse and her father, comfortably ensconced in Flo-

[1] J. Walter in *Plaisir*, Dec. 12th 1945.

rent's magnificent country house. But if we believe that Thérèse has finally accepted happiness with Florent we are rapidly disabused. While her father wallows comically in the creature comforts of soft chairs, fat cigars and fine brandy, rejection of and revolt against Florent's whole privileged lifestyle grow within Thérèse to the point when she makes her famous declaration:

Vous me dégoûtez tous avec votre bonheur. On dirait qu'il n'y a que le bonheur sur la terre. Hé bien, oui, je veux me sauver devant lui . . . (PN.207)

At this point, Thérèse is further from happiness with Florent than at any previous moment in the play. But from this climax, the action changes direction again as under Florent's insistent persuasion Thérèse is drawn back from the brink. She is about to give in when her father enters, grotesque and ridiculous, in a borrowed, ill-fitting top hat and tails. Abruptly her revolt surges up again. This time there will be no going back and Thérèse determines to flee Florent's world immediately. At the last moment, however, she is prevented by a tear from Florent and the curtain falls on a transfigured Thérèse, radiant with happiness, delivered from her sordid past and confident in the future:

et j'ai toute la vie devant moi pour être heureuse. (PN. 235)

The cumulative inevitability of *L'Hermine* and *Jézabel* is gone. In its place we find a greater faith in the inherent dramatic interest and conviction of the main character's psychology and a greater willingness to create theatrical effects from an exploration of its unpredictability. The development of the action is correspondingly more complex. In one sense we have come full circle back to those positive "forward thoughts" Thérèse declared in Act 1. But on the way two key realizations have crystallized in her mind, both of which are central to her final revolt: her rejection of happiness as the world knows it and her perception of the unreality or inhumanity of Florent's world. Although Act III opens with a tableau of Thérèse trying on her wedding gown in the midst of Florent's household, we know it is only a matter of time before she discards it, abandons Florent and returns to the real world outside.

The occasional melodramatic excesses of *L'Hermine* and *Jézabel* are also muted in *La Sauvage*. They are replaced by an admirably sure control of dramatic rhythm and by a finely judged blending of comic and serious. Frantz had remarked in *L'Hermine* that "le drame est un mélange de tragique et de comique". (PN. 118) but this is not borne out by his own play. Frantz also talked of the "sinister farce" to which poverty had reduced his youth. But all this remained imagined and at a remove. The great innovation of *Jézabel* is to give it physical theatrical expression in the form of the hero's family. No doubt Anouilh quickly realized the potential of this for it reappears in several later plays, often entrusted with the major share of the humour. It is this comic function which is most signficant here. Marc's father recognizably prefigures Thérèse's but he is soon sacrificed to the ends of a play concerned with a mother-son relationship. In *La Sauvage*, however, Monsieur Tarde comes into his own. Would-be *bon viveur* and man-of-the-world, his antics in rifling Florent's cocktail cabinet or 'borrowing' expensive cigars, ties and ivory-handled canes are as pitiful and grotesque as they are amusing. His contributions vary from the farcical, through a half-touching, half-comic pathos to more ugly moments when we find it difficult to laugh at all. Anouilh is noticeably attempting not just to juxtapose comic and serious but to overlap and mix them, coming near to the kind of grating effect or *effet grinçant* so characteristic of his later plays. The comic highlight of the second act is Tarde's entrance, dressed in an outrageous borrowed wedding suit: but this encapsulates in one theatrical image the gulf between the two worlds of Thérèse and Florent. In a sense, what we are laughing at is the tragedy of *La Sauvage*.

La Sauvage also possesses considerable poetic qualities which raise it above its two predecessors. Anouilh has told us:

> J'ai refait la pièce plusieurs fois, elle est née peut-on dire par couches concentriques.[1]

That concentricity is apparent in the way all the resources of stagecraft from inanimate objects of the set to costume, lighting and music are harnessed not just to creating a mood but to expressing some of the central ideas of the play. In the last act, all these elements converge at a point in the closing scene. There is a gradual movement from light to dark throughout this act as the evening passes and Thérèse's final rejection of Florent draws nearer. As she goes she leaves behind her wedding dress on the darkened stage which acts as a shining symbol of her sense of purity in a gloomy world. In the background we hear the unsuspecting Florent playing and his effortless mastery speaks more eloquently of the unbridgeable gap between them than could Thérèse's unfinished explanation:

[1] *Le Figaro*, Jan 11th 1938.

Elle murmure, tournée vers le salon où joue Florent comme si elle avait encore beaucoup de choses à dire: Tu sais . . .
Mais elle se détourne brusquement et s'enfonce dans la nuit. La belle robe de mariée reste seule, blancheur éblouissante dans l'ombre. (PN. 272, 273)

Anouilh becomes a proficient craftsman in *La Sauvage*. To some extent this is the natural result of having served his apprenticeship, brief though it was. He was also lucky to have collaborated with one of the great imaginative innovators of the modern theatre, Georges Pitoëff, who produced *La Sauvage*, and whose wife, Ludmilla, played Thérèse. Anouilh recalled their influence on the end of the play "où de coupure en coupure, nous avions fini par ne rien faire dire à Ludmilla qu'un long silence qu'elle disait si bien."[1]

But there is something more in *La Sauvage* which explains the distance between it and the two preceding plays. The absence of melodrama, the sure control of emotion, the blend of comic and tragic, and especially the circumspect and balanced treatment of his themes, all indicate Anouilh's growing intellectual domination of his inspiration. Nowhere in this more apparent than in the rapid evolution of the money theme in this chapter.

For Frantz money seems the solution to all his problems. For Marc it is already doubtful that money alone could erase the taint of his heredity, as son of Jézabel. Moreover, the money ideal is now beginning to seem less attractive in itself. At the end of the play Marc accuses Jacqueline of being, in effect, too good to be true. Her rich upbringing, civilized education and privileged life-style have conferred on her qualities of kindness, understanding, patience and optimism which make her appear superhuman and unreal in Marc's eyes. These are precisely the accusations which Thérèse levels at Florent and around which the inversion of normal values swings in *La Sauvage*. Florent's whole privileged world is criticized for being removed from real life and the play becomes an inverted fairy tale in which Cinderella rejects happiness ever after with her Prince Charming because it would amount to a betrayal of what her past has taught her about the harsh realities of existence.

Anouilh has given us a glimpse of the play's origins which corroborates what we can deduce from internal evidence. It has become commonplace to explain these first plays in terms of Anouilh's own experience of poverty, whether as a child or as a struggling young writer in Paris. Anouilh himself contests this and with regard to *La Sauvage*, in particular, has specified:

[1] Vandromme, op. cit., p. 187.

Je n'aurais jamais écrit *La Sauvage* si j'avais ignoré la condition de pauvre. C'est à travers quelqu'un que j'ai vraiment connu la pauvreté, ce quelqu'un, c'était ma première femme, Monelle Valentin . . . qui sortait d'une vraie misère d'enfance.[1]

It would seem, then, that Thérèse's experience of poverty is not Anouilh's own. It may be no concidence that *La Sauvage* is the first of his plays to feature a girl instead of a young man in the leading role. Taken together, these early works may well be a "théâtre obsessionnel, théâtre hanté"[2] but everything in *La Sauvage* points to Anouilh's growing control over his creative obsessions. The advance from *L'Hermine* to *La Sauvage* is as much an intellectual as an artistic one.

The creative distance between Anouilh and his inspiration creates in turn the preconditions for the most important single development in these years. In *La Sauvage* that theatricality which is obviously instinctive to Anouilh's inspiration and finds expression in *Le Bal des Voleurs* is absorbed into the heart of a serious play. *L'Hermine* and *Jézabel* already contain reminders that we are in the theatre. Frantz, for example, likens his situation to a theatrical one and characters refer frequently to playing their roles and acting out scenes. We must distinguish between this occasional and instinctive theatricality, however, and the issues of these plays—Frantz's choice between murder and losing Monime, Marc's choice between happiness with Jacqueline and his own sordid background—issues which are not seen in theatrical terms. The germ of the idea is there nonetheless. The theme of disgust at a way of life because of its inherent inauthenticity is first broached in *L'Hermine*. Frantz and Monime are already lovers and Monime is pregnant. They must maintain a constant pretence to conceal this from the Duchess. Frantz objects at one point to the lying and deceit in which he has involved Monime but the idea is not pursued.[3] It reappears at the end of *Jézabel* in Marc's reproaches to Jacqueline. In these, as we have seen, Marc accuses Jacqueline of being so perfect that she seems unreal.[4] These, in embryo, are the criticisms Thérèse directs at Florent in *La Sauvage*.

In *La Sauvage* the crucial step forward is taken. Frantz and Marc's intermittent sense of the theatrical is projected by Thérèse onto the world as she sees it and determines the choice she must

[1] *Paris-Match*, Oct. 21st 1972.
[2] G. Marcel, *Revue de Paris*, June 1949, p. 96.
[3] PN. 65–67.
[4] NPN. 115, 116.

make between her own background of poverty and degradation and the happiness offered her by Florent.

There is a remark made by Thérèse in the first act of which few commentators have emphasized the importance. It occurs at that moment mentioned earlier when Thérèse enters to find Florent playing the piano for a solitary drunk. Her eyes are suddenly opened to the gulf that separates their two worlds:

THÉRÈSE: Jusqu'à tout à l'heure — c'est drôle — je ne savais pas. J'étais innocente. C'est eux qui viennent de m'apprendre cela aussi.
FLORENT: Quoi, cela?
THÉRÈSE: Ce que j'étais, ce que vous étiez. (PN. 177)

Thérèse's loss of innocence is, as Hubert Gignoux rightly observes, the realization "qu'un acte n'est pas seulement ce qu'il est, mais aussi ce qu'il a l'air d'être".[1] For the first time Thérèse sees her relationship with Florent through other eyes, as others see it. Her innocence was like that idyllic, self-centred awareness which psychologists tell us is the child's first stage in its developing consciousness of life. Her loss of innocence corresponds to that later stage when the child becomes aware of itself as seen by others. We have here the first explicit dramatization in Anouilh of a peculiar myth in which the birth of self-consciousness and one's subsequent loss of innocence is equated with becoming aware of the theatrical in life. This myth fuses or confuses the two notions of sin and pretence. Henceforth to live or accept a pretence is wrong or 'impure' in the Anouilh terminology. That famous 'purity' which his young heroines struggle to preserve in the face of a degrading world stems from a keenly felt sense of what is authentically themselves. Correspondingly, they reject as 'impure' anything incompatible with that sense.[2]

We can now plot Thérèse's progress. At first ashamed of her sordid past and vulgar family, she comes to see them as a part of all that has made her what she is. This realization places a value upon that knowledge of life's hardships and degradations her past has given her, which in turn devalues the kind of happiness Florent has to offer. The second act brings the pivotal reproach:

tu ne sais rien d'humain, Florent. (PN. 221)

After this there cannot be any permanent reconciliation between

[1] H. Gignoux, *Jean Anouilh*, p. 18.

[2] This concept of purity in Anouilh has many ramifications which cannot be pursued here. It does not mean purity in the usual sexual context, however. The most extensive study of this theme to date is: A. Rombout, *La Pureté dans le théâtre de Jean Anouilh*.

them. It is only a matter of time before Thérèse's revolt wells up again in the third act, against what she sees as the strange pretence of Florent's world, which seems as divorced as he is from real life and all its suffering. This is the great innovation of *La Sauvage*. Thérèse rejects the former ideal of Frantz and Marc as inherently inauthentic and hence incompatible with and unworthy of her personal awareness or conviction of what constitutes her real self. The new balance and circumspection in the treatment of previous themes and the new values in *La Sauvage* proceed from that initial theatricalization of the central dilemma facing the heroine.

La Sauvage then successfully absorbs those self-conscious moments of theatricality which are peripheral and sometimes distracting in the two earlier plays. This solves one problem, however, at the risk of creating another. In the last analysis *La Sauvage* is a naturalistic drama like all of Anouilh's early serious plays. Thérèse is meant to be an intensely real and moving character, caught in a deeply felt dilemma which we are expected to share. Pronko speaks for the majority of critics when he writes:

> Thérèse has all the complexity of a living person . . . Anouilh's portrait of Thérèse is thoroughly convincing and one of the most touching of his entire theatre.[1]

La Sauvage is less monotonously earnest than its predecessors, but even so, its moments of farcical or grotesque humour do not affect the heroine's standing. We laugh, but never at Thérèse. On the contrary, the comedy, along with the play's enhanced poetic qualities, serve to highlight the poignancy of Thérèse's dilemma and increase her emotional appeal.

There is, nonetheless, a latent tension at the very heart of the play. Thérèse is basically a naturalistic creation who becomes theatrically self-aware and who consequently sees the choice facing her in theatrical terms. She is the one real character in the play standing between two equally theatrical and unreal worlds. We have already seen her reasons for rejecting Florent. Although she identifies with her past, she has outgrown it. The characters of her own world are no more than grotesque caricatures as unreal as those of Florent's world and just as unworthy of her keen sense of her own reality. In other words, Thérèse is a character in search of a role which the play apparently cannot provide. The very fact that we can see her predicament in such terms points to the potential contradiction in her position. There is a constant danger that the action

[1] Pronko, op. cit., p. 167.

onstage may explicitly remind us that we are only, after all, watching a character in a role in a play. We already know this, of course, in the back of our minds but reminding us of it is a characteristic of theatre-in-the-theatre and not of naturalistic drama which tries rather to help us forget. In this case the naturalistic appeal upon which Thérèse and the play as a whole depend is constantly threatened.

The success of the play, based for the most part on the personal success of Thérèse, so to speak, suggests that for most spectators the naturalistic illusion has not been spoilt nor its emotional appeal lessened. It is only after the curtain has fallen that we begin to see the possible contradictions in the play. Gabriel Marcel, himself a philosopher, critic and dramatist, remarked that "je ne crois pas que l'ouvrage tienne devant la réflexion".[1] He did not elaborate, but it is tempting to think he had just this aspect of the play in mind.

La Sauvage is the crowning achievement of Anouilh's early work and the finest expression of his naturalistic influences at this stage. At the same time, by assimilating the instinctive theatricality apparent in his early work, it has reconciled for a time two disparate tendencies in his inspiration. But theatricalist tendencies have gained ground and clearly Anouilh has reached the limits of his expansion within a naturalistic mould. We cannot say that Anouilh himself in 1934 perceived things exactly in these terms; but there is no doubt he felt how much of a fulfilment *La Sauvage* was, in theme and technique, because he clearly attempts new directions in the plays immediately following. A new attitude to the theatre is required, to correspond to his growing creative distance from his subject-matter and a new aesthetic approach to express his growing theatricality. Both will come with the writing of *Le Voyageur sans bagage*.

[1] G. Marcel, *L'Heure théâtrale*, p. 92.

II. The Play as Game

Le Bal des Voleurs – Le Voyageur sans bagage – Le Rendez-vous de Senlis – Léocadia

"It is folly to strive for realism under the pretext of creating the illusion of reality."
(Pirandello *Six Characters in Search of an Author*)[1]

Le Bal des Voleurs, written in 1932, is contemporary with *Jézabel* and belongs, strictly speaking, among the plays of Chapter One. We shall consider it here, however, as a preface to *Le Voyageur sans bagage* and to the chapter as a whole. This is really where *Le Bal des Voleurs* belongs, outside the darker inspiration of Anouilh's early plays and not quite with the plays of Chapter Two, although it heralds the spirit of their composition in a remarkable way. It was written, we remember, in imitation of the popular Boulevard comedy of its day. But happily it overshot that modest ambition and was in fact rejected by a number of Boulevard managements.[2] Anouilh looks back upon it now as a seminal work, prefiguring the course and shape of his future writing:

Il me semble que tout est dans *Le Bal des Voleurs*: mes personnages, mes thèmes.[3]

But our present concern is an important discovery Anouilh will make in writing *Le Voyageur sans bagage*, a discovery which will alter fundamentally his view of the theatre and mark his definitive break with the naturalist influences in his first plays. In this respect *Le Bal des Voleurs* is uncannily prophetic. With hindsight we can see the first stirrings of Anouilh's new approach in the attitudes and actions of Lady Hurf, a kindly old aristocrat whose mild eccentricity hides a wealth of wisdom.

Le Bal des Voleurs is a delightful and ever-popular work, full of the exuberance of sheer play. Subtitled a *comédie-ballet*, it unfolds in an atmosphere of theatrical fantasy in which the dialogue is punctuated by music, mime and dance interludes. The three pickpocket heroes of the piece, Peterbono, Hector and Gustave, are doing the summer season at the elegant spa of Vichy, preying upon the wealthy holiday-makers. In fact, they seem to spend most of

[1] From the French version by Benjamin Crémieux.
[2] *Gazette des Lettres*, April 27th 1946.
[3] *Arts*, no. 333, Nov. 16th 1951.

their time stealing from each other under various disguises. This comic ineptitude is compounded by the fact that young Gustave is a struggling apprentice, Peterbono is tiring of the hard life and Hector is dallying with Eva, the niece of a certain Lady Hurf.

Our three pickpockets also have a professional interest in Lady Hurf, or more exactly her jewels, and to pull off this difficult job they decide to disguise themselves as Spanish noblemen. Lady Hurf has more pressing problems, however. She finds Vichy extremely boring and, to make things worse, is being pestered by the Dupont-Duforts, father and son, bankers with their eyes on her nieces' rich dowries. When our most improbable Spanish noblemen appear Lady Hurf seizes the heaven-sent opportunity to amuse herself by 'recognizing' them as long-lost friends and inviting them to stay at her villa.

Lady Hurf performs a number of overlapping functions. She acts by turns as playwright, producer, chorus and spectator of the action. In her playwright role her most important characteristic is a dislike for plots:

il se trame des intrigues: des mariages se préparent. Personellement, je ne peux pas les suivre. Cela me donne la migraine. (PR. 41)

The fact that plots are hard to follow is only a symptom of a deeper malaise. This is that the creative effort required to unravel plots has lost its challenge and attraction, becoming instead a source of boredom:

Moi, je n'y comprends rien et cela m'ennuie au-dessus de tout. (PR. 41)

But in all of this, Lady Hurf occupies a decidedly ambiguous position. Despite her protestations of inadequacy and boredom before the complexities of intrigue, she is the key organizing presence of the play. It is to her boredom that we owe the very *bal des voleurs* itself. Deliberately misreading the announcement of a forthcoming *bal des fleurs*, she has all her guests disguise themselves as thieves for an entirely fictitious *bal des voleurs*. The real thieves make bad imitations while the Dupont-Duforts look so convincing in disguise that they are arrested by the police for a burglary committed by Gustave. Clearly then, Lady Hurf is not loath to create intrigue for her own amusement. There is an important distinction to be made here with *Le Voyageur sans bagage* in mind. It is not the idea of plot itself which stands condemned for an innate lack of interest. The deciding factor is the attitude of the creative imagination to it.

Lady Hurf's attitude stems from one key realization—the futility of existence, which leads in turn to her conviction that life does not necessarily have to be taken seriously:

J'ai cru pendant soixante ans qu'il fallait prendre la vie au sérieux. C'est beaucoup trop. Je suis d'humeur à faire une grande folie. (PR. 43)

Hence her playful approach to life as a means of escaping its seriousness and boredom.

As playwright, we have seen her invent and manipulate intrigue. In her producer role she goes further by illustrating the dramatic process at work, and nowhere more clearly than in her immediate and willing acceptances of the would-be Spanish nobles. This scene shows the foundation of the dramatic illusion being laid. Our disguised pickpockets make highly improbable nobles and Lady Hurf sees through their pretence at once. Nonetheless, she just as quickly falls in with it. In other words, we see an arbitrarily contrived pretence given credibility by a dual and simultaneous acceptance—onstage by the other characters and offstage by the willing complicity of the audience. Here we must remember Lady Hurf's ambiguous position as a character in and spectator of the action. As spectator she knows that the suspension of disbelief requires a deliberate and determined effort. This is one of the basic rules or conditions of the game, without which there can be no 'play'. Hence her impatience with unbelievers like her old friend Lord Edgard who persists in trying to expose the imposters. This impatience is excused by her determination to play the game. Her determination is fired in turn by her knowledge of a darker world beyond the play: for, lastly, Lady Hurf also acts as a chorus. As well as indicating the spirit in which we must enter the game with her, she reminds us of the penalties of not doing so:

. . . Et ce qui est plus grave, je me rends compte qu'entre cette petite fille et cette vieille femme il n'y a eu, avec beaucoup de bruit, qu'une solitude pire encore.

EVA: Je vous croyais heureuse.

LADY HURF: Tu n'as pas de bons yeux. Je joue un rôle. Je le joue bien comme tout ce que je fais, voilà tout. (PR. 65)

Lady Hurf is in fact sketching out the basis of a new approach to the theatre. The plays of Chapter One were serious plays which took life seriously. But Lady Hurf has seen the futility of that and she treats the play as a game. Like any game, we must enter into its spirit and accept its rules and conditions; otherwise it remains meaningless for us. In naturalistic drama it is the playwright who tries to convince us of the reality of illusion. Now it is we, as Lady

Hurf demonstrates, who must make an active and willing contribution to creating the pretence. Can we in return find a release from the seriousness of real living in the theatrical game? If we look to Lady Hurf in this instance the answer is pessimistic. She is the victim of her own lucidity. She can manipulate the game but, by virtue of her privileged position and behind-the-scenes knowledge, she cannot be taken in by the pretence:

Je joue avec le feu et le feu ne veut même pas me brûler. (PR. 65)

But there remain the young lovers of the piece, Gustave and Juliette. While the older Hector and Eva try desperately to re-create their first moment of rapture together Gustave and Juliette, the younger of Lady Hurf's nieces, are falling hopelessly in love. They weather a number of mock-serious tribulations and seem destined to live happily ever after. Through the theatrical game they find true love and each other. As Lady Hurf observes:

Il n'y a que pour ceux qui l'ont jouée avec toute leur jeunesse que la comédie est réussie et, encore, c'est parce qu'ils jouaient leur jeunesse, ce qui réussit toujours. (PR. 130)

There is something fatalistic in this. The world is irrevocably divided into young and old and if one has not received the gift of youth and its concomitant outlook then there is nothing to be done:

Ma petite Juliette, elle, sera sauvée parce qu'elle est romanesque et simple. C'est une grâce qui n'est pas donnée à toutes. (PR. 65)

Only for the chosen and very few then, those who have received the gift of eternal youth, can the game of make-believe supplant reality. The rest of us will always be the victims, to a greater or lesser extent, of our own adult disillusion and lucidity. But *Le Bal des Voleurs* and the type of theatre it presages offer us a challenge. If, for the space of an evening, we can rekindle in our own imagination and sensibilities something of the youthful naivety, simplicity and credulity of the young lovers then we can do justice to the spirit of play which animates *Le Bal des Voleurs* and escape ourselves in the process. That is all its author could wish:

J'ai écrit résolument *Le Bal des Voleurs*. Je suis très fier des éclats de rire qui le ponctuent chaque soir à l'Atelier et je ne m'estimerais pas plus pour avoir écrit une comédie bourgeoise pleine de sous-entendus ou une leçon d'économie politique imagée.[1]

Anouilh himself has pointed to the year 1936 and the composition

[1] Vandromme, op. cit., p. 225.

of *Le Voyageur sans bagage* as a critical turning-point in his career, not simply in terms of professional success, although that came, but because of a profound personal revelation which changed his attitude to the theatre. This was the discovery, in his own words, "qu'un sujet ne se traite point forcément avec sa rigueur naïve, avec sa simplicité ou sa rudesse naturelle, que l'auteur dramatique peut et doit jouer avec ses personnages, leurs passions, leurs intrigues".[1] The fact that this could equally have been said of *Le Bal des Voleurs*, written some four years previously, prompts us to take a closer look at the nature of Anouilh's discovery.

His first plays, *L'Hermine* and *Jézabel* in particular, speak of the frustrations of young manhood:

> Mon impuissance devant le monde . . . où l'on ne peut entrer.[2]

These plays are very much the products of his years of artistic uncertainty and professional obscurity in the early thirties. For love of the theatre Anouilh had given up a comfortable job in advertising to become secretary to the famous actor-manager Louis Jouvet. Disliked by Jouvet, and not the best of secretaries, Anouilh was struggling to maintain a young wife and a new baby, as well as make good his resolution to live only off his writing. It was a time, in his own words, of "une sort de misère café crème et croissants, la misère bohème".[3] The story is told that, at the time of his marriage, Anouilh was so poor he had to furnish his flat with borrowed theatrical scenery and that when his daughter Catherine was born her only cradle was a drawer. Even so, we have seen Anouilh contest the influences of his own early experiences on *La Sauvage*. Critics draw parallels so frequently between Anouilh's first plays and his poverty in the thirties that it is interesting to have his own estimation of it as "la pauvreté bohème, pas tragique".[4] In any case, poverty is relative:

> Je n'ai jamais eu l'impression d'être pauvre, même si je l'ai été. J'ai toujours eu la sensation d'être riche.[5]

This last remark helps underline that we are not dealing with a simple lack of money alone in *L'Hermine* and *Jézabel*, but with a more tangible deprivation, an "impuissance" which it is not difficult

[1] *Les Nouvelles Littéraires*, Jan. 10th 1946.
[2] *Paris-Match*, Oct. 21st 1972.
[3] ibid.
[4] ibid.
[5] ibid.

to relate to a young man's struggle to realize the full potential of his creative promise.

It was thanks to a now forgotten play, *Y avait un prisonnier*, that Anouilh's financial problems were solved. It was only a moderate success on the stage but the film rights were brought by an American producer. The film was never made but Anouilh found a new and unexpected independence and security. This development came on top of a number of other factors, all suggesting that Anouilh had reached a first crossroads in his career. We have seen the personal fulfilment which *La Sauvage* must have been for him. This personal achievement had, by 1934, not been matched by anything like full professional recognition or public success in the theatre.[1] Anouilh had reached something of an impasse. Commenting in 1937 on the success of *Le Voyageur sans bagage*, Anouilh provided a glimpse into his state of mind at this time:

> Le succès m'a un peu inquiété. Je me suis demandé si c'était de bon aloi. Mais le succès m'a aussi encouragé. Le théâtre ne m'intéressait plus.[2]

Such a loss of interest is not surprising in the light of the developments outlined above, and clearly Anouilh was ready for a change. In March 1935, while *Y avait un prisonnier* was in the last days of rehearsal, Anouilh stated clearly and confidently that view of the theatre embodied in Lady Hurf:

> Une représentation théâtrale est un jeu qui obéit à des règles précises. Il faut en accepter les conventions, «conventions» signifiant ici «règles du jeu».[3]

But *Y avait un prisonnier* does not embody the patently new dramatic form which would result from this view and Anouilh must have regarded the play as unsatisfactory because he has never included it in his collected work. It was not until he came to write *Le Voyageur sans bagage* that the full implications of his new attitude were realized in practice. His first attempt at the story produced only a one-act play:

[1] Up to 1936 Anouilh had written nine plays, only three of which had been staged: *L'Hermine* in 1932 (37 performances), *Mandarine* in 1933 (13 performances) and *Y avait un prisonnier* in 1935 (50 performances). After the success of *Le Voyageur sans bagage* in 1937 two earlier plays, *La Sauvage* and *Le Bal des Voleurs*, were produced in January and September 1938. These consolidated Anouilh's reputation.

[2] *Les Nouvelles Littéraires*, March 27th 1937.

[3] *Jour*, March 12th 1935.

Et puis tout à coup j'ai eu l'idée de l'allonger.[1]

There can be little doubt that this extended treatment of the subject was the practical application of his recent discovery. Yet this is not simply a return to *Le Bal des Voleurs* of four years previously. The vital difference is contained in the phrase quoted above: "can and must play". *Le Bal des Voleurs* shows that Anouilh can play. It is a pleasant fantasy and a diversion from the serious mainstream of his early writing. *Le Voyageur sans bagage* marks the realization that the dramatist must play. It is, basically, as serious a work as any in Chapter One but Anouilh chooses to play with his story, his characters and his techniques. It heralds the deliberate adoption of a radically new approach:

L'enthousiasme me revient, maintenant que je sais qu'on peut faire un théâtre artificiel.[2]

This new approach we shall call ludic.[3] Its first effect is to invalidate the premises upon which earlier plays were based. Whereas they had sought to be convincingly realistic, all three plays of this chapter seem deliberately improbable and larger-than-life, even in their basic situations. *Le Voyageur sans bagage* is the story of Gaston, a soldier who lost his memory in the First World War and who has spent the last twenty years in an institution. Several families from different social backgrounds are claiming him as their long-lost son and his self-appointed benefactor, the Duchesse Dupont-Dufort, has chosen the most socially respectable among them for Gaston's first 'home trial'. Her snobbery is well founded because they do in fact turn out to be his real family. The problem is that his real past proves to be very different from what the now naive and inoffensive Gaston had imagined. His *alter ego* Jacques was a brutal and sadistic adolescent, who tortured dumb animals, drank, gambled, embezzled money, crippled his best friend by pushing him downstairs and had an affair with his brother's wife. Faced with these revelations, Gaston resolves to reject a past he nonetheless suspects is his. He is the first to recognize the uniqueness of his position:

Je suis sans doute le seul homme, c'est vrai, auquel le destin aura donné la possibilité d'accomplir ce rêve de chacun . . . (PN. 371)

[1] *Les Nouvelles Littéraires*, loc. cit.

[2] ibid.

[3] 'Ludic' is derived from the Latin *ludus* meaning 'play' or 'game', and describes what is characterized or motivated by a sense of play. A French equivalent exists in *ludique*. The rarity of the word in English gives it a specialized context and helps suggest a more purposeful and serious use of play.

His former mistress, Valentine, offers him proof positive of his identity—the existence of a small scar on his shoulder-blade she inflicted with a hatpin during one of their lovers' quarrels. Gaston discovers this scar privately. Just as he seems cornered, an escape is offered by the appearance of a young orphaned English schoolboy, looking for his long-lost nephew. Gaston seizes upon this entirely fictitious past, denies his real past and the play ends on an optimistic note. The unusual nature of the whole situation invests the play with a peculiar, unreal atmosphere which Hubert Gignoux defines strikingly:

Le Voyageur sans bagage est aux autres pièces d'Anouilh ce qu'une recherche de laboratoire est à un phénomène naturel.[1]

The two other plays of this time share the same basic improbability. *Le Rendez-vous de Senlis* is the story of a married man, Georges, who, in order to impress his new-found love, Isabelle, rents a house on the outskirts of Paris, hires a butler from a catering firm to prepare dinner and two actors to impersonate his mother and father. He invites Isabelle to dinner with the family but with an idealized family, which is a figment of his imagination and far from reality. Georges' play-within-a-play is doomed to failure, however, as the real world keeps intruding on his make-believe. First, his wife attempts suicide and Georges dashes off, leaving two nervous and suspicious actors alone with the butler to greet his guest. Isabelle investigates in his absence and discovers the pretence. Then Georges' embittered friend, Robert, and his wife turn up and Isabelle learns of Georges' real past and present unhappy marriage. But her love is stronger than all because, brushing aside all obstacles, she sits down with Georges and his actors as the play ends to have dinner with the family.

The story of *Léocadia* is, if anything, even further removed from reality. In it another of Anouilh's old duchesses is worried about her nephew, Prince Albert, who is obsessed with the memory of a dead mistress, Léocadia. She has, herself, pandered to this obsession by buying up everyone and everything associated with their brief affair, and transporting them to her château grounds. There she has re-created a totally artificial world in which her nephew can nurture his obsession indefinitely. The Duchess, however, is playing a double game. She has also hired Amanda, a young girl, who is the living image of the dead Léocadia, ostensibly to help the Prince further re-create the past but in the secret hope that Amanda will

[1] H. Gignoux, op. cit., p. 77.

break Léocadia's spell and bring the Prince back to the present. Most of the play is a struggle between Amanda and the ghost of Léocadia for the mind of Albert. Amanda wins of course and falls in love with the Prince, ensuring that everything ends happily, as in the other two plays.

From these brief résumés emerge a number of obvious differences between these plays and their predecessors. Most striking of all is that they end happily. *Léocadia* is almost pure fantasy, closest in spirit to *Le Bal des Voleurs* and anything but a happy ending would be out of place. But even in *Le Voyageur sans bagage* and *Le Rendez-vous de Senlis*, plays with darker moments, a happy ending is contrived. The play is no longer bringing us to a confrontation with harsh reality as in Chapter One, but providing a theatrical make-believe into which we can escape from real life. The intense young hero or heroine of Chapter One has also given way to an older, more mature figure who is looking for a second chance at life and happiness and seems to find it. In keeping with this, the dominant concern of the whole period is the past: how it determines the present and whether or not we can ever escape it. This theme is already familiar from Chapter One, where it was linked to poverty, family and class backgrounds. We shall see it explored here in psychological terms. It will remain one of Anouilh's constant and fundamental preoccupations over the years.

Beneath these immediate differences lie others which indicate a fundamental divergence in outlook and approach between these two chapters. The air of improbability permeating these new plays means that Anouilh has dropped the pretence that a play is anything more than a play. This simple change of attitude is a radical departure from the naturalism of Chapter One. Instead of trying to create a convincingly realistic illusion, the dramatist now frankly underlines the various techniques, conventions and artifices which go into making up a play. The act of artistic creation no longer involves the same seriousness and sleight of hand as before. There is a new mood. It is now a game into which both playwright and audience enter knowingly, willingly and cheerfully. We must now look at the rules and characteristics of this new game. They have far-reaching implications for both author and audience, and for the whole business of writing a play.

The first characteristic of Anouilh's new mood is an expansion of his comic vein. We saw the beginnings of this in *La Sauvage*, where, for the first time, he mixed serious and comic moments, not only to vary mood and rhythm but also to produce a new hybrid tone. This technique now becomes an important expression of the ludic approach. It is a basic condition of this approach that a play's serious moments be muted and any emotional or tragic impact they might have on us be cushioned. As in any game, if we lose our initial lucidity and become emotionally over-involved, then we are playing in earnest, not for fun, and the game ceases to be a game. So Anouilh erects a comic framework to contain these plays' serious elements and maintain a distance between audience and action. The comic or grotesque moments in *La Sauvage* had never detracted from the essential seriousness of Thérèse's dilemma. Now it is precisely this seriousness of the hero's position which is under attack.

The most striking and revealing example of this new technique at work is the brief fourth scene or tableau of *Le Voyageur sans bagage*. Valentine has just told Gaston of the tiny scar which will finally settle the problem of his identity. In the privacy of his bedroom, Gaston removes his shirt, climbs onto a chair, looks at his back in the mirror and bursts into tears. This is a key moment in the play, the modern equivalent of that moment of tragic revelation in the ancient Greek theatre when the hero confronts his destiny. But here the full tragic impact is deflected. The whole episode is witnessed by the butler and valet looking through the fanlight. It is they who relate it to us in their own words. There is already something disconcerting in having Gaston climb onto a chair and the servants, by their reactions, ensure this is not lost on us. Furthermore, the valet's use of a colloquial expression "Y chiale" ("he's blubbering") at once stark and amusing, underlines what is also comic in a tragic moment. The two masks of the theatre are superimposed, creating a new hybrid and ambivalent mood. In constructing this comic framework, Anouilh is indebted to theatre history. He is now noticeably borrowing in these plays from the stock-in-trade of traditional theatre, especially nineteenth-century melodrama. *Le Bal des Voleurs* is already a panoply of conventional situations, characters and routines; but there they are tapped for their native comic potential. *L'Hermine* and *Jézabel* are already melodramatic at times but that is accidental. In contrast, the traditional comic devices and melodrama in these plays serve two purposes. As well as reinforcing the comic framework they also remind us of the artifices of the theatre and underline the ludic process of playing with theatrical conventions.

Valentine's revelation in *Le Voyageur sans bagage*, for example, is not only a *coup de théâtre*. It is also one of the stock recognition devices of popular melodrama whereby countless long-lost and widely scattered fathers, mothers, sons and daughters were reunited onstage throughout the nineteenth century. Similar excursions into melodrama can be found in *Le Rendez-vous de Senlis*. At the end of Act I, for example, when Georges is called away by a theatrically well-timed summons, the play begins to degenerate into a parody of a popular thriller. Two innocent and unsuspecting victims—the hired actors—have been lured to an isolated house at night. The telephone is disconnected. There is a sinister and enigmatic butler and a door "qui s'ouvre toute seule comme dans les pièces policières" (PR. 182). Later in the third act, when Georges' friend Robert arrives and learns Georges' plans from Isabelle, he delivers an embittered and cynical tirade against the melodramatic tendencies of the whole situation. He greets the sudden appearance of Georges' (real) father with:

> Ah! vous voilà vous? Vous arrivez bien. L'atmosphère est tout à fait propice. C'est exactement le moment des apparitions théâtrales. En plein feuilleton, en plein mystère . . . c'est les «Mystères de New York». C'est la frêle et pâle héroïne entraînée toute tremblante par Monsieur dans les plus sombres aventures! (PR. 222)

It should hardly be necessary to point out that this is not real melodrama. Another look at Valentine's disclosure makes this clear. There is indeed a poignant irony in the fact that Gaston's identification with Jacques should be proved decisively by such a trivial, superficial resemblance as a small scar when the real continuities between them lie in the deepest recesses of the personality. This Gaston versus Jacques opposition is very rich in implications for the problem of self-perception, which we cannot pursue here. We ought to recognize, however, that it is in essence one of the comic theatre's oldest conventions—identical twins. We no longer have one 'real' character, as in *La Sauvage*, dominating the play. Indeed, we are prompted to ask: who is the more real of the two, Gaston or Jacques? Gaston is a physical presence onstage who can speak for himself; but he is a thin presence who, at the outset, creates a neutral impression, appearing indifferent and having few convictions of his own:

> Quant au personnage, il n'a pas à être analysé: sa personnalité consiste à n'en pas avoir . . .[1]

Significantly, Gaston's character only fills out as he uncovers Jacques'. He may well protest:

> J'existe, moi, malgré toutes vos histoires. (PN. 352)

but this is precisely what is contested by all the other characters

[1] J. Walter in *Plaisir*, Dec. 12th 1945.

around him, for whom Jacques is more real. By means of this identical twins device Anouilh has distributed between two characters what normally constitutes one single character in the theatre. (We remember how Lady Hurf demonstrated in *Le Bal des Voleurs*, by recognizing the would-be Spanish Grandees, the dual acceptance onstage by the other characters and offstage by the audience, which is basic to the existence of a character.) By doing so Anouilh has moved further from the naturalism of his first plays and tipped the scales towards a thinner, theatricalist mode of character-drawing. At the same time, the contrast between extremes of good and bad in Gaston and Jacques recalls the kind of oversimplified opposition we find in real melodrama between a very good hero and a very bad villain. The fact that Gaston and Jacques are one and the same person, however, makes this conflict tragic and not melodramatic. The real point is that Anouilh is casting a tragic situation in melodramatic terms in order to place a comic and ironic framework between us and the action. This is worth emphasizing because it has not always been understood and has drawn down criticism on Anouilh's head. He has been accused of laziness, lack of invention and of giving up the whole effort of writing a play. It is true that, compared to the tight construction of Chapter One, there seems to be a looser, more nonchalant and even cavalier approach in this period. *Le Voyageur sans bagage* has been dismissed as a mere sketch, with thin subject-matter and no action, which a better writer would have made into a curtain-raiser.[1] This reaction is understandable. Gaston proceeds almost casually from encounter to encounter, unearthing facts about his former self long after we know and he suspects his real identity. *Léocadia* follows the same easy pace and has been criticized for "too many lengthy meanderings with little dramatic justification."[2]

These objections stem from a failure to appreciate the full implications of Anouilh's new attitude. His treatment of his subjects may or may not please, but it must at least be understood for what it is. He is not only keeping us aware of theatre-in-the-theatre, he is attempting to create the impression that a play is not a play. We, the audience, have been freed from the emotional demands of naturalistic drama. What is sauce for the goose is sauce for the gander. The author is now emancipating himself from the constraints of the same theatre. That means throwing off the traditional and seemingly unavoidable burden of writing a play. If it is frankly admitted from

[1] ibid.
[2] E. Marsh, *Jean Anouilh*, p. 90.

the outset that the play is only a game, and if the audience is prepared to enter freely and willingly into the make-believe, then there is no need to invent a complex situation, create and motivate convincing characters and then tease out all the relevant ramifications to a logical and satisfying conclusion. The refusal to do so should not be mistaken for laziness or lack of invention. Anouilh has been unfairly criticized in *Le Voyageur sans bagage* for making things easy for himself by creating an "impossibly good" Gaston and an "impossibly bad" Jacques.[1] But what does it matter since the play is only a play and Anouilh is not trying to convince us otherwise? Just such an opposition of extremes of good and bad provides the required situation and *dénouement*. Anouilh's new approach is a brave attempt to proclaim what he calls "les charmes de la liberté de création".[2]

The various criticisms of individual plays mentioned above are symptomatic of a wider state of affairs in Anouilh criticism. Interest in his well-known themes, such as the search for purity or happiness and the influence of one's past, often obscures the extent of Anouilh's preoccupation with questions of dramatic form. *Le Voyageur sans bagage* is an excellent illustration of this. It is widely and justly admired as a serious drama, and a suggestive and profound study of man's relationship through memory to his past, and of how this affects personality and self-perception. But even admirers are often uneasy about Anouilh's seemingly offhand approach to his subject. In particular he seems to have marred a serious drama by tacking on an improbable happy ending.

There is more unity of design and purpose in *Le Voyageur sans bagage* than this would suggest. As well as exploring the relationship between Gaston and Jacques, Anouilh is just as interested in exploring the nature and limits of his new-found "liberté de création". *Le Voyageur sans bagage* is not the play it seems. At first sight it has all the ingredients of a conventional mystery play. Who is Gaston? Will he recover his memory? What is his real past? But the whole nature of the play is altered by the all-important second tableau. We do not see Gaston at all in this scene. He is in the drawing-room behind closed doors but the assembled household servants, gathered at the keyhole, comment amusingly on his behaviour and reactions. Most significant of all, they identify him positively as Jacques.[3] This revelation colours the development of

[1] P. Thody, *Anouilh*, p. 21. Cf. also Marsh, op. cit., pp. 72, 73.
[2] *Cahiers de la Compagnie Renaud–Barrault*, vol. 26, p. 54.
[3] They might conceivably be mistaken but no one has ever seriously argued this point of view. There is no doubt that their identification is correct and clearly intended as such by Anouilh.

the rest of the play. It neutralizes the straightforward suspense mechanism and allows us, the audience, to observe the action from a distance. This privileged position offers us access to the play's deeper meanings. We can watch Gaston step unwittingly into Jacques' shoes, especially in his scenes with his mother. As Madame Renaud remarks:

Il avait un si mauvais caractère! Amnésique ou non, pourquoi veux-tu qu'il ne l'ait plus? (PN. 361)

It is a central idea of the play that there is something residual in the personality which can survive even total amnesia and makes the possibility of escaping one's past even remoter. One critic has made the fascinating suggestion that Gaston's wilful rejection of his real family at the end of the play is, in fact, a gesture worthy of his former self.[1] Our distance from the action also allows us to play the theatrical game with Anouilh. When, for example, the Duchesse makes a dramatic entrance towards the end of the third scene, to forestall Valentine's disclosure of her decisive proof, we are in a position to appreciate that this is not suspense playing on the emotions of the audience, but rather the dramatist playing with suspense.

Anouilh does more in *Le Voyageur sans bagage* than toy with theatrical techniques. He also strikes a blow for "la liberté de création" by challenging the most immovable of dramatic necessities—that a play must have a beginning, a middle and an end. Where does the play begin and end? The answer depends on what we mean by the play. In a sense it is over with the servants' revelations in the second scene. In another sense it is over in the fourth tableau when Gaston confirms Valentine's proof of his identity. We can, however, date the end of the play to an even earlier moment—to the beginning. There is a very significant remark by the Duchesse to her lawyer in the opening moments:

Ah! non, maître . . . Quelque chose me dit que Gaston va reconnaître ces Renaud pour les siens; qu'il va retrouver dans cette maison l'atmosphère de son passé. Quelque chose me dit que c'est ici qu'il va retrouver sa mémoire. C'est un instinct de femme qui m'a rarement trompée. (PN. 280)

The Duchesse's female instinct is also a thoroughly theatrical one. It underlines and challenges the whole process of our willing suspension of disbelief in the opening moments of the action. In other words it reminds us that a play is only a play by pointing out the

[1] Marsh, op. cit., p. 76.

necessary artifice involved in constructing the initial situation. Of course Gaston will prove to be Jacques, and the Renauds his real family. Otherwise *Le Voyageur sans bagage* as it is could not exist. So the play is over as soon as it begins, with this frank admission that the contrivance of the beginning serves the contrivance of the end. Thus we take our choice of endings, all of them just as contrived as the official happy end. As for the action, Jolivet remarks aptly that "la pièce avance d'une marche rétrograde",[1] that is to a revelation in the fourth tableau which is less a discovery than a confirmation of what we know, the other characters know and Gaston strongly suspects all along. It is hardly surprising that an air of inaction should hang over the whole:

> la facture de la pièce d'Anouilh confine au paradoxe, ne comportant qu'une seule action positive, définie mais non effectuée trois répliques avant la fin.[2]

Le Voyageur sans bagage is a remarkable achievement. On one level it is an absorbing and thoughtful study of the continuity of human personality and the reliability of self-perception. On another level, by a masterly manipulation of levels of impression, Anouilh seems to have written a play without beginning or end, in which nothing happens. In other words, he appears to have avoided writing a play at all! Finally, and most impressively of all, no other dramatic form could better express the central dilemma of a play in which "ses plus humbles gestes ne peuvent être que des prolongements de gestes anciens" (PN. 365).

The same concerns with the practical applications of Anouilh's new ludic stance are evident in the two remaining plays of this chapter. *Le Rendez-vous de Senlis* takes up, in a sense, where *Le Voyageur sans bagage* left off. Whereas we left Gaston about to escape from reality into a fiction of his own choosing, we find Georges in the actual process of trying to create and maintain such a fiction. Of most interest for Anouilh's new approach is a scene in which Georges instructs his two hired actors in how to portray his imaginary parents. Significantly, Georges baulks at the outright caricature of an aged father which the actor Philémon proposes, insisting instead on a portrayal which will not "violenter la nature" (PR. 164). This seems a surprising request in the light of the undisguised theatricality of these plays, but Georges explains his reasons:

> Ces personnages existent. Ces personnages sont déjà à moitié vivants.

[1] Jolivet, op. cit., p. 70.
[2] Ginestier, op. cit., p. 29.

Quelqu'un croit en eux. Quelqu'un attend d'eux certaines paroles, certains gestes . . . (PR. 165)

What Georges is seeking is a compromise—conventionalized characterizations which will serve as frames or outlines, naturalistic enough not to shock an audience's expectations or strain credulity unduly, and which the audience may then fill out and imbue with life according to their own preconceptions. The chief aim of the game is "faire vivre des personnages imaginaires." (PR. 165). Anouilh clearly regards the creation of viable characters as the mainstay of dramatic illusion. In a homage in 1940 to his friend and collaborator, the director Pitoëff, he echoed Georges' words:

vous saviez, vous, que le théâtre c'est d'abord et avant tout DES PERSONNAGES.[1]

For all that, Georges' compromise may indicate some unease or uncertainity on Anouilh's part about the full aesthetic implications of his new stance, and in particular an unwillingness to trust caricatures in main roles. But there is also an underlying ethical concern. Anouilh's new "théâtre artificiel" carried to logical extremes risks becoming nothing more than a gratuitous exercise, for its author's own entertainment, in theatrical artifice and effect. Anouilh clearly does not want this. In another article written in 1940 he argued that the play is an empty and meaningless experience without the participation of an audience:

le public seul lui donne son équilibre et sa nécessité.[2]

The last word is all-important. It is the participation of the audience which converts a gratuitous exercise in technical expertise into a shared human experience and gives it a function and hence an ethical base. Georges is, after all, constructing a pretence into which he can escape, for however brief a time, from the unhappy realities of his life. But, paradoxically perhaps, this pretence must retain some point of contact with real human experience "pour faire croire à une réalité fugitive".[3]

There seems at first sight to be an obvious contradiction between this line of thinking and Anouilh's next play, *Léocadia*, which is the most unrestrained piece of theatrical fantasy since *Le Bal des Voleurs*. But Anouilh's ethical concern with the consequences of his new aesthetic is even clearer in *Léocadia* and the moral of the play

[1] Vandromme, op. cit., p. 187.
[2] ibid., p. 223.
[3] ibid.

in fact belies its obvious theatricality. Prince Albert, we remember, is obsessed with the memory of his brief but intense affair with the extraordinary Léocadia. He is attempting to maintain an illusion, but with little success, because the image he is pursuing is too unreal, unsubstantial and exaggerated to provide a living illusion into which he can escape. Indeed, in a moment of candour, the Prince admits he is forgetting Léocadia:

Je fais tout cela, tout simplement, parce que je suis en train d'oublier, Mademoiselle. (PR. 330)

Amanda is, relatively at least, a flesh-and-blood presence in this static world, an intrusion from the real world outside. Beneath a striking outward similarity she is everything that is antithetical to Léocadia. And the antidote works because she succeeds in the end in drawing Prince Albert out of his nocturnal dream world to face the light of a new dawn. But her victory is ambiguous. In an important exchange, which rarely receives due emphasis, we see Amanda deliberately assume the identity of Léocadia:

Le Prince soupire malgré lui: Léocadia . . .
Amanda tout doucement, comme si c'était elle: Oui, mon amour. Posez vos deux mains sur mes hanches . . . (PR. 371, 372)

If Amanda's presence has infected the Prince's world, the spirit of Léocadia has infected Amanda. She wins the Prince but under the banner of Léocadia and the Prince falls in love with the image of Léocadia in a more tangible, attainable and durable form. He has found an illusion which can withstand the light of day and which is livable and productive. What we are witnessing is not so much the destruction of an image as its transubstantiation. The outward appearance remains, the inner substance is transformed. Albert yields not to Amanda but to Léocadia in Amanda form. The Prince finds then not reality but what Georges was seeking, an illusion with firmer roots in the real which offers a surer means of evasion from reality.

What the story of *Léocadia* amounts to in essence is a critique of Anouilh's new stance. Prince Albert's initial infatuation with Léocadia stemmed from his incurable boredom. Into this "brouillard d'ennui dont je ne pensais jamais sortir" (PR. 354) there came the extraordinary and fantastical Léocadia. For three happy days she taught him how to escape himself and his boredom by playing with life, by not taking it seriously. It is fitting that Léocadia should have been a cerebral figure—"c'était l'intelligence" (PR. 354)—since theatricalism by its lucid, ironic detachment is an attitude more of the head than the heart. But the portrait of Léocadia is also a good-natured, tongue-in-cheek satire of the theatrical approach. This champagne-sipping, orchid-eating aesthete, who strangled herself with her own scarf in the heat of a passionate discussion about Bach, possessed no common humanity. She was caught up in a rarified, élitist, hypersensitive and self-preoccupied literary world into which the hopelessly infatuated Prince was drawn, the somewhat incongruous and hapless victim of his own weakness and his goddess's narcissism.

In contrast, Amanda, the little milliner's assistant, is associated with down-to-earth things and the everyday world of work. The Duchesse's artificial world is peopled with other working-folk, like taxi-drivers, ice cream vendors, waiters and musicians who can no longer practise their trades for real and are tiring of their complicity in maintaining an unreal situation. There is in *Léocadia* a distinct nostalgia for the world of *métiers*. A clear ethical anxiety is discernible in this. The Prince's own forgetfulness and the suggestion that he has to delude himself a little to sustain his infatuation indicates Anouilh's self-criticism. The ludic pose of the artist may be so esoteric and self-preoccupied in nature as to risk divorcing him from the needs and values of the real world.

The answer to this anxiety seems to lie in the substitution of one poetic style for another: the rejection of the unreal and hyperbolic Léocadia for an image with more humanity about it. This does not mean the abandonment of theatricalism. Amanda is still after all a cliché of poetic drama and a far from realistic creation. In the article quoted earlier Anouilh also wrote:

> Je crois simplement que, fuyant le réalisme, sa psychologie étroite, ses larmes et ses éternelles situations, il faut pouvoir jouer d'une façon ou d'une autre avec un sujet au lieu de le subir.[1]

The phrase "d'une façon ou d'une autre" is an important qualification. Anouilh is not reneging on his initial enthusiasm for an "artificial theatre". At the same time, he is obviously unwilling to slip further and further into fantasy. He sees the need to find a dramatic form which, while still appropriate to an artificial theatre, will have firmer roots in the real world. Just as his adoption of theatricalism was to some extent predictable from the developments within Chapter One, so the developments in this Chapter suggest the adoption of a new dramatic form in the plays to come. This new form will be provided by myth.

[1] ibid., p. 225.

III. Tragedy and Myth

Eurydice – Antigone – Roméo et Jeannette – Médée

"Myth alone can preserve the faculties of the imagination from the incoherence of a purposeless activity."
(Nietzsche, *The Birth of Tragedy*).

It is no surprise that Anouilh should turn to classical mythology sooner or later.[1] The modern French theatre has seen a renaissance in mythological drama and several of Anouilh's predecessors and contemporaries had already pointed the way, especially Cocteau and Giraudoux.[2] But why should Anouilh turn to classical models in 1940 and not 1936, the year which marked such a fundamental new departure in his writing? The answer lies, as ever, in a combination of factors. It can be no coincidence that the new violence of tone in these mythological plays coincides with the outbreak of war in Europe. From 1936 to 1939 we had been moving further into theatrical fantasy as an escape from reality. Now, suddenly, in *Eurydice*, as in the other plays of these years, this gives way to a violent, absolute condemnation of all life. Death also makes its first appearance in Anouilh's theatre as an answer to the idealist's dilemma. All the heroes and heroines of these plays choose death in preference to living in a world where their ideals are inevitably compromised and degraded.

Anouilh was mobilized on the outbreak of war and shared in the retreat of French forces in 1940.[3] After the fall of France he continued to live and work in Paris during the Occupation, but took no active part in the Resistance, as did Camus and Sartre, for example. Nonetheless, no writer could hope to insulate himself entirely from

[1] This chapter also includes one play, *Roméo et Jeannette*, which is not based on classical mythology. The famous couple alluded to in the title, Shakespeare's Romeo and Juliet, are, however, as much a part of the mythology of love as Orpheus and Eurydice. Moreover, we shall see that this play is so important an indication of Anouilh's changing outlook in these years that it could not be displaced from the sequence.

[2] Cocteau formed part of Anouilh's adolescent reading. His gift was the first revelation of a modern *poésie du théâtre* Anouilh had not imagined. Giraudoux was a stronger, formative influence. Anouilh was so overcome by the stylistic beauty of *Siegfried* in 1928 that he wept. He claims to know the play by heart and has often spoken of his debt to Giraudoux. Cf. Vandrome, op. cit., pp. 167, 191.

[3] Anouilh dramatizes some of these experiences in a more recent play, *Les Poissons* rouges (1968). Cf. *Radio Times*, July 9th–15th 1977.

the emotions and events of such a period and these present plays no doubt reflect the tenor of their violent and gloomy times. Wars and their aftermath all too often mark the boundaries of historical periods. We shall see that these plays of the war years form a critical stage in Anouilh's thinking and bring to a close the first broad phase of his evolution.

This change cannot be attributed wholly to external factors, however. Anouilh is clearly also refining his thoughts on that conflict between idealism and reality which has been the nucleus of his drama to date. From the outset his heroes and heroines have been doomed to unhappiness and prevented from realizing their ideals both by the weight of their own pasts and by the inevitable compromises needed to live in an imperfect world. In the plays of Chapter One, and again in *Le Rendez-vous de Senlis*, this failure was linked to social factors. In *Le Voyageur sans bagage* social obstacles were removed and the determining influence of one's past was explored on the psychological level of memory and the personality. As Anouilh reflects on the problems, he is finding even deeper reasons, intrinsic to human nature and life itself, for the failure of idealism in the world.

This is enough to explain the pessimism and sense of predestination which pervades this chapter. These in turn help explain why Anouilh should graft his own preoccupations onto mythological frameworks. By doing so he takes a step further into theatricalism. We recall that Anouilh's earliest heroes were occasionally afflicted by a self-consciously theatrical view of themselves as role-players. This sense of life's theatricality now becomes all-embracing. Not only is the play a play, all the world is a stage and all its men and women are players, acting out their alloted roles in the age-old, endlessly repeated story of life. Three of the present plays are based on familiar myths from classical antiquity. We know the characters, the stories and the outcomes. This knowledge overshadows the action in each case and a sense of predestination prevails as we watch the characters act out their parts to the preordained conclusion. Likewise in *Roméo et Jeannette*, although it is not based on a classical myth, the title indicates that its young lovers will not find happiness in this world.

This knowledge of the outcome puts us the audience in a privileged position, which suggests the final reason why Anouilh should look to mythology at this point. Just as his ludic approach was to some extent predictable from the developments within Chapter One, so his use of myth is an answer to the anxieties of Chapter Two. There we saw Anouilh's growing ethical concern to justify his enthusiasm for a poetic theatre in terms of human relevance. Myth would appear to offer an ideal solution. It is "an abstract or purely literary world of fictional and thematic design, unaffected by canons of plausible adaptation to familiar experience".[1] In that respect it obviously forms an ideal basis for a poetic, non-realistic theatre. At the same time, because of its special nature and significance, it remains relevant to all men and all ages in a way that perhaps no other poetic restatement of the human condition could. We are then simultaneously distanced from the action by our foreknowledge of the *dénouement* and involved in those fundamental truths about ourselves which myth enshrines.

Dramatizing well-known stories also enables Anouilh to continue from Chapter Two another prerequisite of this ludic approach to the theatre, underlining the essentially artificial nature of the whole dramatic process. The mythological characters of these plays, in particular, are by definition literary or dramatic fictions since each is an integral part of its own story and since they exist in our mind not as real people but as fictions. Their reality depends on the very fact that they do not have to try to be realistic. They are known to be, and accepted as, mythological figures. This in turn allows Anouilh to remind us of the artificiality at the heart of characterization. The whole process of creating logical, reasonable or sufficient motivation between characters and their actions is after all as much an agreed convention of the theatre as anything else. Although it is this motivation which makes characters appear real and independent, in fact, it serves the author's intentions and the purposes of the story he has written. *Antigone* turns the whole process of normal character motivation on its head. It is a naturalistic drama in reverse in which the main character is progressively stripped of all the normally credible reasons for her conduct. Antigone appears fully-fledged at the beginning of the play having already accomplished the act which will be her undoing. In defiance of her uncle Créon's royal edict, she has performed funeral rites over her rebel brother Polynice whose body Créon has left to rot outside the walls of Thebes. She justifies herself at first on the grounds of sacred duty and sisterly love, but as the play progresses she is forced to admit the absurdity of her act and of life itself. Antigone's true and only reason for acting as she does is herself. She is after all Antigone and we know that it is Antigone's allotted role from time immemorial to defy Créon to the bitter end. She is only a character in an age-old story, compelled to act out her role every time that story is

[1] N. Frye, *Anatomy of Criticism*, p. 136.

retold. On the thematic level this expresses Anouilh's sense of predestination and the theatricality of life. On the aesthetic level it lays bare the mechanism of dramatic necessity. All the rest, character motivation included, is a game the author plays with his public's notions of what is logical, plausible or probable.

All in all, then, myth provides Anouilh with a continuing basis for a poetic and artificial theatre. It allows us to participate lucidly in the theatrical game and, as in Chapter Two, the onus of conviction lies on us, not on the dramatist. We participate willingly or not at all.

As in the previous chapter, however, a failure to recognize or accept this challenge has led to misunderstanding and criticism. In this instance, his handling of myth has caused a good deal of adverse comment. His modernization of the stories, in particular, has, in the opinion of many, been the cause of stylistic lapses and inconsistencies, trivialization of the characters' motives and a general cheapening of the significance of his original material. *Eurydice* is a case in point. Some praise it for the richness of its thought and the excellence of its poetic writing, while others denigrate it as an unsuccessful hotch-potch of styles, too realistic to be mythical, too symbolic to be naturalistic or too naturalistic to be poetic.[1] The play is not, like *Antigone*, based on a Greek original and Anouilh takes more liberties with the myth. Orphée is a busker who travels about with his old father, living off pennies from café terraces. Eurydice lives an equally nomadic and obscure existence as an actress in a provincial repertory company. They meet towards the end of the first act on a railway station platform when Eurydice is drawn to the sound of Orphée's violin. They introduce themselves as Orphée and Eurydice and their immortal story begins.

They go off together to Marseilles, where a first shadow is cast over their love by the sordid hotel room in which it is consummated and by the thought that countless other anonymous couples have used the same room for the same actions and gestures. More, Orphée's idealistic insistence on the need for absolute honesty between them makes Eurydice realize that their love cannot survive in the world. Like other Anouilh heroines, she knows some of life's harsher realities and her past is far from unsullied. She decides to leave Orphée and, in the process, is killed in a road accident. The third act is the most mythical or fantastic of the play. Through the offices of a mysterious figure, Monsieur Henri, who dogs the lovers' foot-

[1] Harvey, op. cit., p. 84; Ginestier, op. cit., p. 51; Pronko, op. cit., pp. 134, 199; Marsh, op. cit., pp. 105, 106.

steps, Eurydice is restored to life and reunited with Orphée in the deserted, eerily lit station café. Again, however, Orphée proves incapable of compromising with life. Insistent on knowing the truth about Eurydice's past relationships, he disobeys Monsieur Henri's injunction not to look her in the face. Eurydice 'dies' once more, this time for ever. In the last act it only remains for Orphée to be persuaded by Monsieur Henri and the spectacle of his degraded old father that life is not worth living. He goes off to commit suicide and be with Eurydice for eternity.

The same modernization is apparent in *Antigone*, although on a more limited scale. This play has seen many varied productions but its original, intended setting—and undoubtedly the best—was a neutral décor comprising three identical doors leading off from a central acting area in which the action took place. This stylized representation of a Royal palace achieves a degree of sparseness and abstraction which contrasts forcibly with the evening dress worn by the principal characters and the black leather trenchcoats worn by Créon's guards. What offends most sensibilities, however, is not costume but the blatant anachronisms in the text. It seems a cheap trick, pointless and unworthy of the legend, to have a king of ancient Thebes speak naturally of cigarettes, nightclubs, guns and sports cars while his guards discuss central heating and family allowances. In fact, the really significant difference between Anouilh's *Antigone* and that of Sophocles is Anouilh's emphasis on childhood. Whereas the heroine of Sophocles' play sacrifices herself for the highest religious motives, Anouilh's Antigone harks back constantly to the happy, innocent, idyllic world of her childhood and, in a famous rejection of life and happiness, exclaims:

> Vous me dégoûtez tous avez votre bonheur! Avec votre vie qu'il faut aimer coûte que coûte . . . Moi, je veux tout, tout de suite — et que ce soit entier — ou alors je refuse! . . . Je veux être sûre de tout aujourd'hui et que cela soit aussi beau que quand j'étais petite — ou mourir. (NPN. 188)

This emphasis has reduced Antigone, in the eyes of many, to a wilful, stubborn, unreasonable adolescent who simply refuses to grow up. Their sympathies are with Créon, who accepts life as it is, rolls up his sleeves and gets on with the dirty business of politics and government, not with an Antigone who seems to lack the tragic grandeur of her Sophoclean original.

Similarly in *Médée*, Anouilh appears to have imposed his own interests to the extent of creating a totally self-preoccupied and unsympathetic heroine whose death is an act of deliberate and vengeful self-destruction. This play concentrates on the best moments of the Medea story, as told by Euripides and later Seneca. Anouilh's Jason and Medea are *gitanes*, the kind of timeless gypsy figures whose caravans have roamed Europe for centuries. When the play opens Jason has already abandoned Médée. Tired of their itinerant existence, he is attracted as much by the settled life of nearby Corinth as by its young princess Créuse. Médée, alone in her encampment with her nurse and children, plots her horrific and famous revenge. She sends a poisoned wedding gift which kills Créuse and her father Créon, cuts the throats of her two innocent sons, sets fire to the caravan containing their bodies and before Jason's eyes throws herself into the inferno.

The remaining play, *Roméo et Jeannette*, despite the absence of a classical ancestry, has not been spared. It has been dismissed as highly melodramatic and improbable, criticisms which are not far removed in spirit from the objections to Anouilh's treatment of myth. This play is the story of two lovers, Frédéric and Jeannette, who like their Shakespearian counterparts fall in love in impossible circumstances. The enmity between the houses of Montagu and Capulet becomes in Anouilh a clash of two completely different lifestyles. Frédéric, solicitor son of solid country bourgeois stock, arrives with his mother and fiancée Julia to meet his future in-laws. Julia, Frédéric and his mother are of the same race—prim, proper and industrious; but Julia's family, in contrast, turns out to be unconventional in the extreme. Her father is an indolent, easy-going retired artiste, her brother Lucien is an embittered cynic who is separated from his wife, and her younger sister Jeannette is a sluttish child-of-the-forest whose relationship with a rich neighbour Azarias provides the family income. Frédéric's mother is predictably appalled. There is no one to meet the visitors, the house is a shambles, no one has bothered to prepare lunch. Indeed the money Julia had sent in advance had been squandered in the local pub. In this improbable setting the improbable happens. Frédéric and Jeannette fall in love. Like the lovers in *Eurydice* they run away together but, because of bad weather, get no further than an abandoned cabin in the forest where they are forced to spend the night. Meanwhile, in despair, Julia attempts suicide. Frédéric, hearing this, returns to her. Jeannette ripostes by marrying Azarias. In the last act the visitors are preparing to return home, with the sound of wedding celebrations in the background. As they drive off, Jeannette is spotted walking into the sea in her wedding dress. Suddenly Frédéric leaps from the car, runs to join her and the two lovers walk hand-in-hand to their death.

Anouilh is doing what dramatists have been doing for centuries. He has taken a number of pre-existing stories and adapted them to express his own interests and preoccupations. We see several characteristic Anouilh themes emerge in these plays: in *Eurydice*, the idealist's stubborn refusal to accept any kind of compromise with life; the same in *Antigone*, motivated by a powerful nostalgia for lost childhood innocence; In *Médée* the heroines efforts to redeem her real self after years of dependence on Jason; in *Roméo et Jeannette*, love's failure to survive in the world. In keeping with Anouilh's intentions and subject-matter, different plays exhibit different degrees of modernization. It would not be difficult to justify Anouilh's treatment of myth in each individual case and answer specific stylistic criticisms individually. This is neither possible nor necessary within the scope of the present study. It is more interesting and instructive to see specific objections in the general context of what Anouilh is trying to achieve in these mythological plays, and counter them in that light.

There is, moreover, implicit in these various objections to details a more fundamental and far-reaching criticism which can only be answered in general terms. It is that the combined result of Anouilh's handling of myth is that "ultimately the myth itself becomes contingent."[1] In other words, Anouilh has chosen to use myth in the first place as a means of expressing his sense of universal predestination. But the subsequent freedom and individuality he allows his characters, whose motives and actions are more familiar to Anouilh's theatre than to Greek mythology, seem to invalidate any symbolic and tragic force these myths may have. The net effect is that "the inevitability of the tragedy thus becomes subordinate to an inherent trait in the character."[2]

This is an interesting argument because, like other mistaken criticisms of Anouilh, it at least directs our attention to an important area of his thought or practice. There is indeed an apparent inconsistency between Anouilh's recourse to myth and his presentation of the characters he finds there. This is not a fault or a contradiction, however, but a deliberately induced tension between the characters and their roles. This tension is in turn an accurate transposition onto the stage of our participation as audience in the unfolding dramatization of the myth and, outside the theatre, of our relationship to the fixed and known form of our own existence.

Mythological drama works at two levels. On one level there is

[1] Grossvogel, *The Self-conscious Stage*, p. 185.
[2] ibid., p. 181. Cf. also Thody, op. cit., p. 34 and Gignoux, op. cit., p. 95.

the-myth-in-the-making—that is, the familiar story as it is retold from moment to moment, action to action, event to event. On another level, while this process of retelling is going on, there is ever-present the idea of the finished story as a completed whole, that entity which we call 'the Antigone myth' or 'the Medea story' and so forth. As we watch the play unfold we witness the gradual convergence of these two levels as each action or event is woven into the completed pattern. Our minds are thus moving constantly between these two levels and, in this respect, the performance of the dramatized myth becomes a model of the human consciousness of existence. It re-creates in the theatre that constant oscillation from particular to general, from fragment to completed pattern which characterizes life itself.

We have the same dual perspective upon our own lives as upon the mythological play. The form or outline of our lives is fixed and known to us just like these ancient stories. We can view our lives in this long-term perspective and watch a preordained pattern of birth, maturity, decay and death moving towards fulfilment. But if we lived our lives entirely in this way and allowed this view to dominate our minds the logical outcome would be total resignation, passivity and inaction. Of course, we do not, because we also have a short-term perspective which enables us to live life from day to day, getting and spending, pursuing aims and ambitions, as if we were unaware that our 'story' will end inevitably in death—indeed, almost in the paradoxical hope that it may somehow end differently. We participate in life as we participate in the dramatized myth, living both to the full from moment to moment, despite our certain knowledge of the outcome.

We could almost say that we exist in a state of tension between the two perspectives mentioned, both in the theatre and in real life. It is this tension which is expressed in Anouilh's seemingly inconsistent handling of his characters. Their relative freedom or independence within the fixed form of their stories represents the only freedom that we can have in the face of our own destiny. Seen in this light, Antigone's momentary recantation is not a structural flaw in the play and does not constitute "an inconsistency . . . between Anouilh's view of tragedy as pure fatality and the moment of free choice which he gives Antigone".[1] Faced with her stubborn refusal to see reason, Créon reveals that the disfigured body lying outside the gates of Thebes could equally well be that of her brother Étéocle and not of Polynice. Political necessity required a hero and a

[1] Thody, op. cit., p. 31.

villain, so from their two unrecognizable corpses on the battlefield Créon chose one for a state funeral and left the other to rot. It mattered little, moreover, since both brothers were in fact traitors and were both planning to overthrow the government. Shaken by this glimpse of political realities, Antigone abandons her defiant insistence on burying Polynice. For a little while it seems that she will agree to live, marry and grow old like everyone else. Then, irked by Créon's mention of the hated word 'happiness', Antigone's revolt wells up again and she reaffirms her choice of death in preference to life. Far from being a flaw, this hesitation is a significant incident. It creates in the audience a moment of paradoxical suspense which derives from that tension between the idea of the myth in its completed form and the myth-in-the-making, discussed above. Although we know it is impossible, Antigone seems nonetheless to have halted or reversed the course of her destiny. Perhaps the story will end differently after all.

Of course, it does not and cannot because we are powerless to alter our destinies. In this respect our freedom is illusory. Even so, we are thinking beings who can at least see beyond our own ultimate helplessness and imagine states of existence not subject to our imperfections and limitations. If nothing else, this is proof of an independent and self-conscious intelligence which is not completely subordinate to the forces of blind determinism. To that extent we enjoy a real freedom, if only to perceive and interpret the world in which we find ourselves and the meaning of our existence in it. In other words, we cannot alter the general outlines and outcome of the myth or story of life but we are at least free to interpret its meaning.

There is, then, no real contradiction between Anouilh's using myth to convey a sense of universal predestination and the subsequent liberties he takes with it, especially in the area of characterization. Each time the myth is re-enacted, we are free to read it anew and differently, just as each age and generation of mankind sees the world through fresh eyes and discovers the meaning of life again for itself.

This very freedom poses another aesthetic problem which threatens to undermine the assumption that myth is relevant; but again it is one to which Anouilh is sensitive and of which he is aware, well before his critics. If each age thus reinterprets the myth of existence, what guarantee is there that an audience will find any points of reference in a poetic theatre based on myths from classical mythology? This in fact raises far-reaching issues which, although stemming from Anouilh's own preoccupations, are relevant to the wider effort in twentieth-century theatre to find a satisfactory dramatic form to express the modern tragic sense. To tackle them we must turn to one of Anouilh's finest and most famous plays, *Antigone*. It lies at the heart of this period because it is a test-case for many of the issues raised by Anouilh's recourse to myth. It is also the play in which aesthetic questions are most thoroughly absorbed into the very theatrical form of the play itself and, for that reason, most often neglected.

Antigone is the only one of his plays which Anouilh has explicitly labelled a tragedy[1] and yet it would be hard to find a work whose worth and standing as a tragedy has been more frequently contested. Many see it as Anouilh's one and only masterpiece, a marvellous fusion of ancient and modern elements, in which the timeless confrontation between the idealism of youth and the pragmatism of age is stated in balanced, essential and universal terms. Others dismiss it as a mixture of cheap sentimentality, facile anachronism and gross caricature in which there is no tragic conflict at all. In fact, in *Antigone*, Anouilh is himself as concerned as his critics with the basic question of what constitutes tragedy.

The chorus of the play offers one, now famous view of tragedy. Antigone's attempt to bury Polynice's body has been discovered. A very nervous and apprehensive guard reports this act of defiance to Créon, who immediately institutes an inquiry. At this point the Chorus intervenes:

> Et voilà. Maintenant le ressort est bandé. Cela n'a plus qu'à se dérouler tout seul. C'est cela qui est commode dans la tragédie, on donne le petit coup de pouce pour que cela démarre . . . Après, on n'a plus qu'à laisser faire. On est tranquille. Cela roule tout seul. C'est minutieux, bien huilé depuis toujours. (NPN. 160, 161)

This view of destiny, characteristic of a mechanized age, is familiar from Cocteau's *La Machine Infernale*, to which Anouilh is doubtless indebted. Antigone would subscribe to this view inasmuch as she comes to us having already accomplished that act of defiance needed to set the tragic mechanism in motion and hoping to acquiesce in the inevitable fulfilment of her role and destiny. She sees herself as a tragic heroine and shares the Chorus's abhorrence of that other, adulterated and unattractive genre, the *drame*. Tragedy, says the Chorus, is clean, restful and sure. There is no hope of escape and we have only to accept the inevitability of death. The *drame*, on the contrary, is full of the trials of persecuted innocence

[1] Harvey, op. cit., p. 93.

and of the struggles of heroes and villains, traitors and avengers. It thrives on suspense and the ever present hope of last-minute escape, with the result that "cela devient épouvantable de mourir, comme un accident" (NPN. 161).

The progress of the play-in-the-making, however, neither supports the Chorus's definition of tragedy nor helps Antigone act out her tragic vision. It does not resemble an efficient and well-oiled mechanism. Antigone has yet to confront Créon, who does not wish to help her accomplish the inevitable. On the contrary, he is a character from the *drame* inasmuch as he hopes to find a way out of what is for him a political embarrassment by some strategem or compromise. Indeed, as we have seen, he almost succeeds for a moment in deflecting Antigone from her purpose. Faced with this hesitation, we are tempted to think, as the Chorus suggests we might in the *drame*:

On aurait peut-être pu se sauver . . . (NPN. 161)

The fine engineering of the *machine infernale* is not as smooth, restful and reassuring as the Chorus would have us believe. Significantly, Antigone describes the progress of the action and her confrontation with Créon in terms more reminiscent of the Chorus's definition of the *drame* than of tragedy.[1]

The play itself, then, is an obstacle both to the Chorus's mechanistic conception of destiny and to Antigone's vision of herself as a traditional tragic heroine. Initially she poses as the heroine of a Sophoclean tragedy, expropriating many of the characteristics of the original Antigone. She defends her action on the grounds of fraternal love, family obligations and the observance of sacred rite. But from the very beginning Antigone finds herself in a different play-world from that of her Sophoclean model. She has to contend with problems of love and sentimentality not found in the original play. Entering for her first scene, she finds not her sister Ismène, but her childhood Nurse. This leads to a touching and sentimental episode not in Sophocles. Shortly afterwards, she is drawn into a love scene with Créon's son Hémon which, again, is not in Sophocles. None of these characters shares her sense of tragic destiny: they all want her to live.

There is, then, a significant discrepancy between Antigone's view of herself as a tragic heroine and the reality of the situation in which she finds herself. The implications of this discrepancy have not always been appreciated. Her insistence on burying Polynice, for

[1] NPN. 188.

example, is explained by the ancient Greek belief that "ceux qu'on n'enterre pas errent éternellement sans jamais trouver du repos" (NPN. 169). The retention of this ancient motivation has been criticized as illogical beside the twentieth-century anachronisms which litter the play.[1] The disparity is deliberate. Antigone's motives are inherently implausible in the twentieth century and are meant to seem so. In a crucial exchange Créon discredits these motives as absurd and meaningless and Antigone admits it.[2] The modern play is unfolding in an absurd world where the gods are dead and where sacred rite has degenerated into meaningless ritual. The world has outgrown the barbaric, heroic times of its youth. Créon is no run-of-the-mill tyrant but a modern head of state. Étéocle and Polynice are not mythical heroes but "deux larrons en foire qui se trompaient l'un l'autre en nous trompant et qui se sont égorgés comme deux petits voyous qu'ils étaient, pour un règlement de comptes" (NPN. 184). The modern world is one of political deception, expediency and compromise, of clashes of material interests and worries about petty self-advancement.[3] Antigone must act out her tragic role in an environment devoid of the appropriate grandeur and sobriety of tone and in which the values of ancient tragedy are meaningless, even for the heroine herself.

Antigone cannot then be a replica of the Sophoclean tragedy. The Greek Antigone could live and die as the champion of religious values and divine justice. She found a meaning in life and death which was derived from beyond them. The only ultimate value the modern Antigone can assert is herself, in the face of an absurd destiny. Créon asks for whom or for what cause she persists in an absurd defiance. Antigone replies:

Pour personne. Pour moi. (NPN. 174)

In place of the values of the ancient tragedy Antigone offers us two 'solutions' to living in an absurd world. We may adopt Créon's position, but this is a short-term solution which fools no one, least of all Créon. He accepts the role in which events have cast him, at the head of the Theban government. Furthermore, he accepts the inevitable compromises, unpleasantness, dishonesty, ruthlessness even, of the job precisely because Fate has placed him there and the job must be done. He has no illusions about the ultimate absurdity of life but his practical, constructive approach confers a form and meaning on life from the inside, as it were. It is each

[1] Thody, op. cit., p. 33.
[2] NPN. 172–174.
[3] NPN. 159, 164, 197–199.

individual's destiny to die but mankind as a whole survives. Créon sees life as a communal experience. He maintains the ideal of public order and he cheats death by creating enduring structures based on the continuance of society and civilization. On the survival of the species Créon builds an illusion of order, permanence and purpose in the Chaos.

Antigone views life as an intensely individual experience and, in the absence of external absolutes, she turns in upon herself. She dies to be true to this self. She confronts her destiny by changing it from 'Death' to 'my death'. Paradoxically, she attempts to defeat the absurdity of having to die by willing it, insisting upon and going to meet it in a "tête-à-tête avec le destin et la mort". (NPN. 170). Arguments will continue as to which of these attitudes is the more admirable, worthwhile or heroic. But ultimately both Antigone and Créon are pleading the same case. Both are trying to justify a meaningless existence in an absurd world and make some sense out of having to die. They differ in proposing two instinctive and irreconcilable solutions.

Which of these is the more heroic, the more tragic—a young girl's passionate rejection of life or an old man's stoical and disillusioned acceptance? Is the modern *Antigone* more or less a tragedy than the Sophoclean original or has Anouilh's modernization of the myth precluded the possibility of any tragedy at all? There can be no final and certain answers to such questions because we cannot separate what appears tragic in the theatre from our sense of what is tragic in life. By virtue of this very relationship, the criteria for any literary *genre* cannot be fixed and stable things. In the end, terms like tragedy and *drame* lose all point as value judgments and those who judge *Antigone* from prior conceptions of what a tragedy ought to be neglect the aesthetic side of the search by Anouilh's idealists for purity and absolute values. It is difficult to apply fixed classifications to a play about the relative, shifting nature of all such classifications. *Antigone* is a play in search of standards and values; a tragedy in the process of re-definition.

This search for standards—aesthetic as well as ethical—in *Antigone* epitomizes the character of this period as a whole. It is a crucial stage in Anouilh's evolution; one in which his outlook and values begin to alter fundamentally. Previously his theatre had been dominated by his idealistic heroes and heroines, and life seen through their eyes had been found wanting because it did not match up to their demanding standards. Now condemnation of life's imperfections begins to give way to tolerant understanding of the compromises needed to live in society and even to a realization that accepting life with all its imperfections and getting on with it can be just as heroic in its own way as sacrificing oneself for an unattainable ideal.

In *Eurydice* the balance of forces is still on the idealist's side. The last act is devoted entirely to confirming this. Here suicide does indeed seem preferable, as Monsieur Henri insists, to the "absurd melodrama" of life, illustrated by the antics of Orphée's old father—ludicrous attempts at Swedish gymnastics, pathetic self-satisfaction and libidinous daydreams of exotic beauties rolling cigars on their thighs. Even if this spectacle of life's inevitable degradations finally justifies Orphée's intransigence, there is nonetheless a cruel and inhuman side to his idealism. It is, after all, his uncontrollable need to know the truth about Eurydice's past which, despite her poignant pleas to be allowed to live, 'kills' her again in the third act. More importantly in the long run, Orphée's idealism also misleads him into loving an idealized image of a perfect Eurydice who does not exist in reality. Idealism then can be not only inhuman and cruel, it can also be self-deluding. It is precisely these traits which, stiffened and accentuated, will be used to caricature the idealist in *Colombe* and the other plays of the fifties.

In *Antigone* arguments for and against the heroic attitude are evenly balanced. Antigone's self-sacrifice is a universal protest at lost innocence and perfection which strikes a chord in all of us, even if we do not share her determination to die. But Créon's arguments in favour of accepting life as it is and getting on with the job are both reasonable and persuasive. Moreover, when he extols the humble joys of living—a good book, a child playing at one's feet, relaxing on a bench on a pleasant summer evening in front of one's house—he too awakens a response in us. Destiny has cast Créon in the unheroic role and Antigone in the heroic one, but he achieves a grandeur of his own which cannot be meaningfully measured against hers. They are two alternative, instinctively felt views of life and heroism and we are left to choose between them.

After *Antigone* the balance tilts in favour of accepting life, and self-sacrifice is felt as an increasingly pointless and wasteful solution. Nowhere is this clearer than in Anouilh's treatment of his young lovers in *Roméo et Jeannette*. In *Eurydice* Orphée's intransigence is finally justified by the "absurd melodrama" that is life. In *Roméo et Jeannette* this melodrama is turned against the lovers. The play has often been criticized over the years as exaggerated and melodramatic. In fact, the melodramatic elements are intentional. As in *Le Voyageur sans bagage,* Anouilh is treating serious matters in a melodramatic way in order to distance us from them and curb our sympathies. This process is most obviously at work during the lovers' abortive idyll in the third act. We recall that Frédéric and Jeannette have gone off together at the end of the previous act. But they are caught in a storm and forced to shelter for the night in a lonely, abandoned cabin in the forest. This is the setting for Act III. It is a highly conventionalized situation in itself—two runaway 'children' taking refuge in a remote cabin in the forest. It is also hedged about with melodramatic effects. From the moment of Lucien's entrance and his mocking remark:

Un drôle de temps pour une idylle (NPN. 302)

their love scene is doomed. He brings a wedding veil from Jeannette's lover, Azarias, and she is caught out in a lie she has told Frédéric earlier, about how she obtained the wedding dress she has brought with her. Jeannette counters with a melodramatic effect of her own, by slashing her arm on a broken window pane to prove her love for Frédéric. But before this can take effect there is yet another theatrical apparition. The Postman arrives with the equally dramatic news of Julia's attempted suicide, which snatches Frédéric away from her and back to her sister. The lovers' idyll *Eurydice* was just as short-lived but it was not so parodied. That is the all-important difference. The lovers are reunited in death at the end of the play but this, too, is not presented straightforwardly. It is the morning of Jeannette's marriage to Azarias and Frédéric, now reconciled with Julia, is on his way home with her and his mother. Suddenly, he spots Jeannette in her white wedding dress, walking across the sands towards the incoming tide. He jumps from the car and runs to join her. They embrace and are engulfed in the rapidly rising tide. This walk into the sea is somewhat extravagant in its own right but any tragic impact it might have on us is further muted by the presence of Jeannette's old father. Anouilh leaves it for him to relate the episode to us as it happens and deliver a grotesquely funny commentary on their last moments in the world.[1]

Despite this treatment we can still feel some sympathy for Frédéric and Jeannette, victims of a world in which true love is inexorably doomed. In *Médée*, on the other hand, it is Jason who, despite strictly speaking his desertion and betrayal of Médée, emerges as the sympathetic character in the end. Médée's assertion of her true self, after years of compromise, becomes a destructive and revengeful monomonia which involves her innocent children and alienates her audience. As Jason says:

[1] NPN. 344–348.

Personne n'aura jamais pitié de toi . . . L'homme Jason te juge avec les autres hommes. (NPN. 382)

Jason, humbly and reasonably, pleads the same case for living as Créon and the balance of the argument has now shifted in his favour. This argument is moreover couched in terms of an opposition between two races of people and two lifestyles. Monsieur Henri defines them in *Eurydice*. One is that numerous, happy, fertile race of everyday folk who eat and sleep, work and save, year in year out, and who, despite wars and epidemics, seem to go on for ever. The other is the noble race, the heroic few who want to experience life to the full, with all its perils and rewards, who can just as easily end up triumphant between a guard of honour or condemned between two *gendarmes*.[1] These individuals are, by definition, an élite, outside the mainstream of ordinary life; but as this period progresses their activities and preoccupations are increasingly seen as a threat to civilized life. Simultaneously the everyday folk grow in prominence and importance. The final *envoi* of Médée, for example, is left to two minor characters, the Nurse and the Guard. While Médée was holding forth we had no time to heed them but, as the Nurse affirms, "j'avais pourtant quelque chose à dire" (NPN. 398). That something is an acceptance of ordinary, unheroic living and its humble joys. There is even a note of hope for the future. In the Guard's words:

Il y aura encore du pain pour tout le monde cette année-ci. (NPN. 399)

What will this future be in terms of Anouilh's development? The impulse towards an ideal is an intrinsically dynamic force. This dynamism can be judged for good or for ill. In these years it is seen as increasingly destructive and futile. When Frédéric forsakes Julia for her wild child-of-the-forest sister, it is the loss of order and stability he feels most:

Le monde avait une forme avant, bonne ou mauvaise. (NPN. 339)

Conversely, when Jason deserts Médée, it is in the hope of returning to the ordered world Frédéric has left:

Ce monde, ce chaos où tu me menais par la main, je veux qu'il prenne une forme enfin. (NPN. 388).

Here we have the clear expression of a growing wish for new standards and a new stability in a period of changing values and lost ideals. It is also clear what this new scheme of values will be based

[1] PN. 470.

on. The former, humble everyday folk will become the new heroes of Anouilh's theatre. The childish absolutism of earlier plays will be replaced by a mature acceptance of life and a lucid awareness of its ultimate absurdity.

This evolution is bound up with a new importance attached to the idea of *métier* or work. Créon, we remember, emphasized the need to accept one's job, whatever it might be, and do it to the best of one's abilities. Jason takes up this same theme. He speaks of erecting his "pauvre échafaudage d'homme" (NPN. 398) and of his "mur dérisoire, construit de mes mains entre le néant absurde et moi" (NPN. 390). What this attitude proposes is, in fact, a new function and value for the theatre. The dramatist's *métier* and the frail man-made structure he erects is, of course, the theatre. It is the theatre itself which is now envisaged as filling the vacuum left by the devaluation of former ideals, giving a new shape or form to life and standing between man and the ultimate absurdity of existence. But Anouilh's theatre itself must change form to express his new altered vision of things. We must look to the plays to come for the elaboration of this new form and function.

IV. L'Invitation au Château

"Les hommes, n'ayant pu guérir la mort, la misère, l'ignorance, ils se sont avisés, pour se rendre heureux, de n'y point penser."
(Pascal, *Pensées*)

"On trompe la mort en empêchant de penser à soi." (Anouilh)

The changes we have seen taking place in Anouilh's outlook and values within Chapter Three bring to a close the first broad period of his evolution. Anouilh himself clearly realized this. André Frank reports a confidence made early in 1946:

je m'arrêterai d'écrire pile pendant deux ans. J'abandonnerai mes personnages à leur jeu. Je chercherai pour mon théâtre une nouvelle voie.[1]

A number of reasons have already been suggested to explain Anouilh's adoption of myth and the dark, pessimistic mood of Chapter Three. In this immediately post-war period other factors emerge to confirm the change of outlook already taking place.

This time was not an entirely happy one for Anouilh personally. It is not an invasion of his privacy to note, some thirty years on, that his marriage to Monelle Valentin was not destined to last much longer. The problems of the couple obviously loom large in three of the plays in the preceding chapter and some of those close to Anouilh at the time suggested that Lucien in *Roméo et Jeannette* who has a cynical, fatalistic attitude to love, was the character "qui correspond le mieux aujourd'hui aux préoccupations d'Anouilh."[2] We shall find the same emphasis on the couple and their problems and the same pessimism about love in the plays of the late forties and early fifties.

Another significant contributing factor to Anouilh's state of mind at the time was the post-war *épuration*, "un moment où la France a été ignoble".[3] Anouilh was repelled by the vengeful nature of much of the justice meted out after the Liberation, when undoubtedly a lot of old scores were settled. His reaction to the death of

[1] *Gazette des Lettres*, April 27th 1946.
[2] André Barsacq in *Le Spectateur*, Feb. 11th 1947. Cf. also Gabriel Marcel in *Les* Nouvelles Littéraires. Dec. 12th 1946.
[3] Anouilh in *Paris-Match*, Oct. 21st 1972.

Robert Brasillach in particular had a profound and lasting effect upon his outlook:

La mort de Brasillach m'a bouleversé.[1]

Brasillach was a novelist, dramatist and critic whose pro-Fascist sympathies earned him enemies during the Occupation. After the war he gave himself up to the authorities and was duly tried and condemned for collaboration. His case has attracted attention again in recent years. At the time it became something of a *cause célèbre* among writers and intellectuals of whom some, François Mauriac, for example, made pleas for clemency on his behalf. Anouilh helped gather signatures among his peers for a petition and the difficulties he encountered doing this left him disillusioned and bitter. Brasillach was executed on the sixth of February, 1945. In fact, Anouilh hardly knew Brasillach and, reading his recollections of the affair, written down in later years,[2] one comes away with the feeling that Anouilh was defending not just Brasillach but himself and his own vision of the world:

J'étais très pur à trente ans: la rigueur, c'était quelque chose pour moi.[3]

The Brasillach affair seems to have been, in Anouilh's eyes, a last chance for the world to redeem itself and show itself worthy of the high ideals of his young heroes and heroines. Brasillach's death marked the death of a part of Anouilh's hope for the world:

Le jeune homme que j'ai été et le jeune homme Brasillach sont morts le même jour et — toutes proportions gardées — de la même chose.[4]

The events and the issues of the Liberation made a lasting impression on Anouilh and there are clear echoes of them in *Becket, Pauvre Bitos, Les Poissons rouges* and other plays. He developed a number of specific political antipathies at this time—for example, a dislike of De Gaulle—but the main effect of these disillusioning experiences was to diminish further the standing of the hero in his plays and corroborate the growing relativism of standards and values in the plays of his middle years.

All of this seems a far cry from *L'Invitation au château* which is a delightful theatrical fantasy, full of wit, charm and comic invention, in the vein of *Le Bal des Voleurs* and *Léocadia*. Horace and

[1] ibid.
[2] Vandrome, op. cit., pp. 175–179. The Brasillach affair is discussed on pp. 115–118. Cf. also E. de Comminges, *Anouilh, littérature et politique*, pp. 91–94.
[3] *Paris-Match*, loc. cit.
[4] Vandromme, op. cit., p. 175.

Frédéric are identical twins, dressed alike for good measure and played throughout by the same actor. As one can imagine, this leads to several moments of enjoyable confusion. Horace, however, is unhappy. His brother, the gentle Frédéric, is hopelessly infatuated with the rich, spoilt and wilful Diana, daughter of the all-powerful financier Messerschmann. Irritated by this unlikely match, Horace has devised a plan to break Diana's hold over Frédéric. He hires Isabelle, an attractive young dancer from the Opera, who, he hopes, will outshine Diana at a forthcoming ball. The plan succeeds admirably until his aunt, Madame Desmermortes, another of Anouilh's aristocratic old ladies, decides to annoy her nephew by taking a hand in the deception, and introducing Isabelle's mother to the ball as a highly improbable 'Countess Funela'. Faced with this threat to his schemes, Horace reacts by revealing all and destroying the illusion he has himself created. It is left to Madame Desmermortes to patch things up. In her wisdom she unites Frédéric and Isabelle, who are obviously made for each other, and reconciles Horace and Diana, who have just as obviously been in love throughout.

No *résumé* could do justice to the many subplots, superbly funny moments and admirably engineered scenes of this play. Nor can it be fully appreciated in isolation because it in fact teems with familiar Anouilh characters and themes. It is indeed a 'cocktail' of a play,[1] in which Anouilh seems to take stock by mixing together many of the staple ingredients of his theatre. To take a few examples, Isabelle is a direct descendant of Amanda in *Léocadia*, the other Isabelle in *Le Rendez-vous de Senlis* and Juliette in *Le Bal des Voleurs*. Madame Desmermortes is also immediately familiar as one of those old aristocratic ladies, aunts or duchesses, who are constantly interfering in his plays, plotting behind the scenes and taking things into their own hands when the theatrical game threatens to turn sour.

Some themes we might more readily associate with more serious plays also emerge in *L'Invitation au château*. Most notable is the money theme from *La Sauvage* in Chapter One, which plays a substantial part here. Messerschmann is used to buying compliance but, despite his vast wealth, he cannot make his own daughter Diana happy. Money cannot win Horace's love nor help her outshine Isabelle's natural beauty. Her father attempts to bribe Isabelle into leaving but when Isabelle simply refuses his money and decides to leave for nothing, Messerschmann's whole scheme of values comes crashing down around him. In a memorable scene he and Isabelle

[1] Ginestier, op. cit., p. 85.

sit on the stage gleefully tearing up hundreds of banknotes. As in *La Sauvage*, money does not bring happiness and Messerschmann is inwardly one of the unhappiest characters in the play.

In fact, beneath the theatrical high spirits, the underlying vision of life is just as bleak as in Chapter Three. Messerschmann observes gloomily:

On est tout seuls, voilà ce qui est sûr. On ne peut rien les uns pour les autres, que jouer le jeu. (PB. 126)

We are still actors on the stage of destiny in *L'Invitation au château*, condemned to act out our allotted roles in a play in which death is the only and inevitable *dénouement*.

The presence of these darker themes in a theatrical extravaganza like *L'Invitation au château* has left many critics puzzled and uneasy. There is unanimous admiration for the impressive technical achievement it undoubtedly is. But for some this is its only substance:

There is little in it besides a complicated plot and entrances and exits arranged with the precision of a ballet.[1]

Others point to the more sombre thoughts in it but hesitate about how seriously to take them in this highly theatrical context.[2] For at least one critic this unresolved tension between form and content dooms the play to failure.[3] This state of affairs is yet another example of looking for a play's message or ideas elsewhere than in the whole of its dramatic form. *L'Invitation au château* may well be "a pleasantly jumbled fairytale"[4] but it is also a highly significant work, occupying a pivotal position between the early and middle periods of Anouilh's theatre. It shares the same preoccupations with the form and function of the drama that characterize all of Anouilh's work. We shall see that there is no tension or contradiction between its bleak vision of life and its theatrical exuberance. On the contrary, form and content are directly linked. Playing for the fun of it can be a way of playing in earnest.

Let us begin by looking at Horace and Frédéric, the two characters around whom the play revolves. They represent, as Horace acknowledges, "la plus mauvaise convention théâtrale" (PB. 39)—

[1] D. Knowles, *French Drama of the Inter-War Years*, p. 174. Cf. also Vandromme, op. cit., p. 112; Marsh, op. cit., pp. 135, 139; Thody, op. cit., p. 42; Della Fazia, *Jean Anouilh*, p. 78.
[2] C. Borgal, *Anouilh: la peine de vivre*, p. 106; Thody, op. cit., p. 43; Pronko, op. cit., pp. 124, 150.
[3] Radine, *Anouilh, Lenormand, Salacrou*, p. 43.
[4] Della Fazia, op. cit., p. 78.

the identical twins device which is as old as comic theatre itself and out of which playwrights have long ago squeezed every laugh and comic effect imaginable. Nonetheless, a look at the function and implications of this convention will lead us directly to the real meaning of *L'Invitation au château*.

Horace and Frédéric are physically indistinguishable but they differ significantly in temperament. Horace defines this difference: "Il s'est fait entre nous un partage. J'ai eu autre chose, il a eu tout le cœur" (PB. 72). What is Horace's "autre chose"? Frédéric suggests part of the answer:

Il est très intelligent, bien plus que moi. Très courageux aussi, très intrépide . . . (PB. 69)

In short, Frédéric is the passive and acquiescent twin. Horace is active and "intrepid". Frédéric is also naive, romantic and sentimental. Horace, in contrast, is lucid, intelligent, disillusioned and somewhat cynical. Horace's ambitions are in keeping with his intrepid character. He is prepared to take upon himself the responsibility for his own destiny and that of others for the duration of the play. He explains to Isabelle:

Nous sommes trop négligents . . . Je comprends cela en politique. Il faut se laisser gouverner comme on se laisse couper les cheveux — par d'autres, tant bien que mal . . . Mais permettre au destin de vous conduire . . . cela, c'est grave, mademoiselle, c'est impardonnable . . . Je ne me sens pas d'humeur à supporter l'ordre normal des choses aujourd'hui . . . Alors tant pis pour la fatalité! . . . Je prends tout sur moi et je brouille les cartes. (PB. 40, 41)

The reasons for Horace's battle with destiny are several. He is simply bored for one thing, a fact which reminds us of Lady Hurf's resort to play as an escape from boredom in *Le Bal des Voleurs*.[1] A more pressing reason is Frédéric's infatuation with Diana Messerschmann. Horace is annoyed by this unlikely liaison which is an attraction of opposites. He is particularly irritated by Frédéric's sentimentality and naive lack of insight into Diana's real character. It is also a relationship which, in Horace's estimation, is doomed to failure and Horace has a declared physical aversion to all that is, or threatens to be, a failure.[2] But there is one paramount factor which gives Horace the right, in his own eyes, to assume the role and responsibilities he does. He claims to be the only one with the detachment and lucidity necessary to direct the game he plans:

[1] Compare PR. 43 and PB. 132.
[2] PB. 135.

Je n'aime personne, mademoiselle. C'est ce qui va me permettre d'organiser en toute sérénité d'esprit la petite comédie de ce soir. (PB. 40)

Moreover, when Madame Desmermortes decides to upset her nephew's schemes by introducing Isabelle's mother into the proceedings, Horace reveals a cruel and vindictive streak in his nature. He gets up on a chair, interrupts the ball, denounces the pretence he has himself carefully created and ridicules the assembled guests for their credulity in accepting "la caricature réussie de votre propre parade" (PB. 100). Initially, he had intended to fight like with like, and dull Diana's brilliance by presenting Frédéric with an even more resplendent Isabelle. Now that this plan is threatened, nothing less than the total destruction of the illusion will satisfy him. It is left to Madame Desmermortes to gather up the disentangled threads of Horace's plotting and contrive a happy end. One of those "vieilles femmes qui commencent à y voir clair" (PB. 145), she in fact has the lucid insight which Horace would like to possess but she tempers it with the "heart" of Frédéric. She is in a position both to manipulate the game with more success than her nephew and to bring it to a satisfactory conclusion:

Tout doit finir bien, c'est convenu. (PB. 152)

Madame Desmermortes embodies one of the oldest and most reassuring conventions of comic theatre: the happy end.

If all this is not just "a pleasantly jumbled fairy tale" what does it mean? To begin with, the identical twins Horace and Frédéric correspond to two aspects of one and the same creative sensibility. In particular, they represent two conflicting tendencies in Anouilh's own inspiration which are apparent throughout his work. We have seen Anouilh's interest in and borrowings from theatrical tradition, both comic and melodramatic, in Chapter Two. Just as some of his characters yearn for the innocent, secure world of childhood, Anouilh himself has often confessed his own fondness and preference for a traditional, escapist theatre full of the magic of an uncritical submission to the illusion. He suffers, in his own diagnosis, from "une obscure nostalgie des rideaux rouges qui tombent"[1] which cannot be unconnected with his own first contacts as a child with the magical, larger-than-life world of nineteenth-century operetta.[2] Frédéric stands for this regression towards a more innocent type of theatre and the temptation to acquiesce in a naive and sentimental vision of the world. Horace, on the other hand, is the active and

[1] *L'Avant-Scène Théâtre*, no. 372.

[2] Cf. Anouilh's recollections in *Paris-Match*, loc. cit.

organizing intelligence of the play, the builder and destroyer of illusions. His impulse to control and dominate the course of events cannot allow him to accept a romantic, superficial view of the world. If Frédéric represents the tendency to sentimental self-indulgence, Horace represents a corrective, self-disciplining reflex. He shares two characteristics with Anouilh: a craftsman's aversion for what is lax, uncontrolled and potentially flawed, and a self-conscious fear of ridicule.[1]

What was true, then, of previous plays, for example *Le Voyageur sans bagage*, *Léocadia* and *Antigone*, is true also of *L'Invitation au château*. Beneath the obvious concerns of each we find the same continuing preoccupation with aesthetic matters. Here Anouilh is dramatizing two different sides of his own inspiration. We are not, however, asked to choose between them because it becomes a three-cornered debate with the intervention of Madame Desmermortes. It is she who resolves the conflict and, in the process, defines a use and function for the theatre at this important stage in Anouilh's evolution.

Madame Desmermortes is as lucid and intelligent as her nephew, if not more so. Her clear-sightedness comes of a long experience of life and it retains a human concern; witness her efforts to unite the young lovers at the end. Horace's code of behaviour is purely pragmatic and does not concern itself with questions of good or evil.

MADAME DESMERMORTES: Nous nous retrouvons là tous les deux, tout bêtes, sans être sûrs d'avoir très bien agi.
HORACE: Bien agi, mal agi . . . Vous en êtes encore là? Vous m'étonnez ma tante. Je vous croyais beaucoup plus forte. (PB. 133)

For Horace the important thing is to act, to do something to upset the seemingly inevitable progress of destiny, regardless of the fact that people may be hurt in the process. *L'Invitation au château* has been a challenge to his intelligence and powers of improvisation; but, quite apart from the fact that he has not met the challenge with entire success, the attempt has produced, in Madame Desmermortes' view, only a display of impressive but sterile, technical virtuosity. Technical brilliance is not true beauty because it lacks heart. Madame Desmermortes disillusions Isabelle about Horace:

On n'est jamais si beau que cela, mademoiselle, quand on n'est pas très humain en même temps. Ce n'est pas tout d'avoir de jolis yeux, il faut

[1] Anouilh's pride in his craft is proverbial. Cf. *Opéra*, March 7th 1951; *L'Avant-Scène*, Dec. 15th 1959. He admits his fear of ridicule in *New York Times*, Sept. 13th 1964; *Paris-Jour*, Sept. 8th 1969.

qu'une petite lampe s'allume derrière. C'est cette petite lueur qui fait la vraie beauté. (PB. 142).

In other words, the technical achievement must have a human dimension and it is on this basis that Madame Desmermortes makes sure that all ends well. In doing so she reconciles not only the two sets of young lovers but also the conflict between Horace and Frédéric. In her, a lucid appreciation of reality coexists beside the hope that something can be done to make life tolerable and perhaps even happy:

Nous braillons les uns à côté des autres sans nous entendre et sans nous voir, et nous disons: c'est le désert! Heureusement qu'il existe encore quelques vieilles femmes qui ont renoncé à cette folie pour leur compte et qui commencent à y voir clair, à l'âge hélas, où l'on met des lunettes. (PB. 145)

L'Invitation au château is taking up where Chapter Three left off. There we saw the growing value attached to accepting and doing one's job as well as possible, as one way of giving some purpose to living in an absurd world. From the dramatist's point of view, this outlines an ethical basis for the theatre. *L'Invitation au château* makes it clearer what the theatre's new function will be.

In the long term we cannot remedy the absurdity of life, we cannot choose not to be born and we cannot stop our inexorable progress towards our ultimate destiny—death. Even the enterprising Horace acknowledges this:

Je trouve l'homme trop modeste. Il se laisse mener alors que c'est presque toujours à lui de décider et qu'il est pratiquement indomptable. L'amour, la maladie, la bêtise, il a trouvé commode d'appeler tout: fatalité. Moi, je ne connais que la mort. (PB. 40, 41)

At the same time, Horace also clearly refuses to submit to all the other apparent "fatalities" which affect our lives in the short term. In this lies Anouilh's function for his theatre and the new value he attaches to his craft. We cannot avoid death; but, if we can forget ourselves and our worries by playing the theatrical game, we can at least escape for a time from the feeling of relentless progress towards death:

ISABELLE: Ah! monsieur Horace, c'est mal de ne penser qu'à jouer!
HORACE: On a juste le temps de cela, ma chère, avant d'être tout à fait mort." (PB. 101, 102)

Anouilh's nostalgia for traditional comic theatre and his interest in its oldest and most enduring conventions are an integral part of this function he envisages for the theatre. By accepting and using this tradition Anouilh sets his own activities as a dramatist in a long historical perspective which further adds to the value of his craft. Mankind has, from time immemorial, transposed reality into comic and conventionalized terms. He has created in the theatre an alternative, timeless world in which he can laugh at his own absuridty and ineffectualness and in which things always turn out all right in the end. The theatre itself is becoming the "mur dérisoire" of which Jason spoke between himself and the ultimate absurdity of existence.

It is this view of the theatre's function which unites content and form in *L'Invitation au château*. The vision of life may be bleak but an antidote to it lies in the comic form of the play. This is also the real significance of *L'Invitation au château*. At a crucial time in Anouilh's development, on the threshold of a new period in his writing, it reaffirms a function for the theatre and a value for the playwright's *métier*. Implicit in all this is an ethic of endurance not of rejection and self-sacrifice as before. The world is no better a place than before; indeed, it may be the poorer for the absence of its young heroes and heroines. But it is there and life has now to be lived. The theatre, by helping us laugh at ourselves, offers the possibility of some reconciliation with the harsh realities of life and the chance of a respite from them which gives us the courage to go on.

V. The Farce of Life

Ardèle – Colombe – La Répétition – La Valse des Toréadors

"Ce qui fait frémir contient de quoi faire rire."
(Ghelderode, *Hop Signor!*)

The present chapter spans the years 1948 to 1951 and contains four major plays.[1] This short but crowded period seems at first sight to be a mixed one. No single type of play characterizes it as easily for us as in Chapter Three for example. *Ardèle* and *La Valse des Toréadors* are, in Anouilh's terminology, *farces grinçantes*. *La Répétition*, on the other hand, is an elegant, polished *comédie brillante* and *Colombe*, while belonging to the same collection of *Pièces brillantes*, has much more in common with the two farces.

Beneath the obvious differences of approach and form these plays do have enough in common to constitute a recognizable group and stage in Anouilh's development. We have now entered a period in which, as the Count in *Ardèle* observes, "rien n'est si simple" (PG. 55) and where the all-or-nothing attitude of Orphée or Antigone is no longer acceptable. The dominant mood is one of mature disillusion with the outlook, values and ideals of earlier years. Indeed, mature is the key word because a fundamental shift of viewpoint has taken place in Anouilh's work. From the outset his theatre has been dominated by his young heroes and heroines and it is through their eyes that we have seen the world. The focus is now that of adulthood and middle age and it is through older, wiser eyes that we now view the idealism of youth. Where young lovers or idealists still appear they are relegated to minor roles. They are touchingly innocent but hopelessly naive and inexperienced beside their worldly-wise elders. A new type of principal character becomes the centre of interest. He is middle-aged or older, unhappily married and, while not forgetting the hopes and inspirations of his youth,

[1] There are also two shorter works, *Épisode de la vie d'un auteur* (1948) and *Cécile ou l'école des pères* (1949). The former was produced as a curtain-raiser with *Ardèle*. It tells of the everyday trials and tribulations which interrupt a writer's creative efforts. The latter is an enchanting *divertissement*, almost a period piece, in the manner of Molière, with touches of Marivaux. It was given privately on the occasion of Anouilh's daughter Catherine's wedding in 1952, with the bride herself in the title role.

has experienced at first hand the inevitable disillusionment of age.

The best embodiment of this new ambivalent mood, and the most amusing, is the retired General around whom both farces revolve and who will reappear in the next chapter. General Saintpé (or Saint-Pé) has not forgotten the stirring, heroic times he had as a young cavalry lieutenant but finds issues in the present domestic and marital world much more complex and insoluble than on the battlefield. He can be blunt and forthright in typical military fashion, but mostly his attempts to call a chaotic and insubordinate household to order end in comically ineffectual bluster. There are other moments of poignant regret and lucid self-depreciation which are genuinely moving; but, for the most part, he has learned to compromise with life and accept the limited pleasures and consolations it offers. These are mostly sexual, it must be said. Love and sexuality figure prominently in this period as a whole, in which we find the same preoccupations with the male-female relationship as in Chapter Three. Anouilh's convictions have not altered, only his viewpoint, which is now that of the older couple Jason and Médée rather than of the young lovers Orphée and Eurydice. Life still has the same degrading, disillusioning effect on love as on all other human ideals. Whereas Orphée and Eurydice, Frédéric and Jeannette had chosen to die rather than experience that effect, the protagonists of these plays have lived. Their experiences only confirm the pessimism of their younger counterparts. The General in *Ardèle* explains to his young daughter-in-law Nathalie:

Il y a l'amour bien sûr. Et puis il y a la vie, son ennemie. (PG. 14)

This terse observation is a leitmotiv for this whole group of plays.

The one character in this period who most resembles the heroes of before is Julian in *Colombe*. He is a man of such rigid principles that he chooses to live in poverty with his young wife and child rather than ask his famous actress mother for support. Called up for military service, however, he is forced to swallow his pride and entrust his family to his mother's charity and to the tender mercies of the facile, hypocritical and immoral theatre world he abhors. During his absence his wife Colombe makes her début on the stage and discovers an unsuspected talent. Julien also makes a discovery—that she is being unfaithful. He returns to confront her and discover her lover's identity. It turns out to be none of the backstage Lotharios who traditionally prey on young actresses but his own brother, Armand. Julien is totally uncomprehending and, in one striking dramatic moment, kisses Armand himself in a helpless attempt to understand how Colombe could be attracted to him. The gulf between Julien and Colombe is unbridgeable; all the more so now that a selfish and self-preoccupied side of Colombe has emerged with her new-found success in the theatre. Their relationship is at an impasse and the play ends in a poignant flashback to their first meeting. The little florist's assistant, Colombe, enters the theatre with a large basket of flowers for Julien's mother. She meets Julien and, attracted by his ill-temper and mulish pride, chooses to go off with him rather than accept a part in the current play. It is love at first sight and, they believe, forever.

One of the lasting fascinations of this play is the complex and shifting balance of sympathies between Colombe and Julien. They blame each other of course and accuse each other of selfishness, and they are both right. Certainly another Colombe, spontaneous, pleasure-loving, self-centred, with a remarkable facility for pretence emerges after exposure to the theatre world. But this Colombe has always been there and the Colombe Julien loves—pure, proud, staunch companion in idyllic deprivation—is largely a fiction of his own imagination. The interesting lesson here is that the defeat of idealism comes as much from within the hero himself as from the world outside. Like Orphée, Julien is blinded by his own total rigidity and unreasonable intransigence. Indeed, in Julien idealism is stiffening into something self-deluding, mechanistic and possessive. This leaves the hero himself open to caricature and indeed Julien is halfway between character and caricature. The part he wants to play in life is not the part that circumstances force upon him. He returns from the wars, as it were, in Act III to confront a faithless wife but the dramatic, moving scene he intends never materializes. Life is a *farce grinçante* and it has cast him in the traditional farce role of the deceived husband. Moreover, farce keeps intruding upon this scene. It takes place in Colombe's dressing room and Julien's indignant reproaches are repeatedly interrupted by the various comical fauna of the backstage world, coming to warn Colombe of her husband's imminent arrival. Julien's outraged honour seems increasingly incongruous and more to be laughed at than sympathized with.

This view of life as a tragi-comic farce is the *raison d'être* of *Ardèle* and *La Valse des Toréadors*. In *Ardèle*, the earlier and shorter of the two, General Saintpé makes his first appearance. This play is a tale of the love of two hunchbacks. One is the Ardèle of the title, middle-aged spinster sister of the General. The other is her music teacher, with whom she has at last found true love. The General has convened a family council of war to deal with the situation. His other married sister, the Countess Liliane, arrives with her husband the Count and her lover Villardieu, both of whom are identical in dress and appearance. Their various attempts to reason with Ardèle, who has barricaded herself in her room and never appears throughout, form the substance of the play. While they pass judgment on a liaison they deem grotesque, it is in fact their own relationships which are judged. These prove to be just as grotesque in their own way. The General is tied to a demented invalid wife, literally insane with jealousy, who calls his name regularly every quarter of an hour to check on his movements. He snatches what physical comfort he can, where and when he can, with the maid. The Count is burdened with a demanding young mistress, lodged at a nearby inn. Villardieu, jealous of the Count, spends sleepless nights watching Liliane's bedroom while she, jealous of her husband's mistress, watches the Count's, who thus rarely gets to see his mistress. This farcical and embroiled situation is brought to an abrupt and tragic climax by the suicide of Ardèle and her lover. The last word of the play is left to the General's two precocious children Toto and Marie-Christine. Dressed in grown-ups' clothes, they scream protestations of mutual love and batter each other. They are a grotesque travesty not only of adult relationships but of Anouilh's own earlier theme of childhood innocence.

Ardèle has predictably offended and disgusted some people over the years, not because Anouilh made his lovers into hunchbacks but because love itself seems to have degenerated in this play into animal instinct. When the General's wife suddenly bursts from her room at the end it is to deliver a demented tirade against a world of universal, nightmarish sensuality:

> Je peux te dire la minute. Je peux te la dire pour le chien qui va dans la cour de la ferme, la nuit, chercher la chienne en chaleur; je peux te dire le jour où on amène le taureau au village et toutes les bêtes des bois, sous la terre, dans les herbes, dans les arbres . . . Et les belettes et les blaireaux et les fouines et les renards dans la clairière et les insectes, les millions d'insectes, en silence, partout. Tout jouit et s'accouple et me tue . . . Tous ignobles, vous êtes tous ignobles avec votre amour. Le monde est ignoble et il n'en finit plus. (PG. 79)

Even the General's young daughter-in-law Nathalie, who at first sight seems to be another of Anouilh's pure young things, has grown up and discovered the sensuality within herself. Economic necessity forces her to abandon her childhood sweetheart Nicolas and marry his elder brother. She tells Nicolas of her wedding night:

> quand il m'a prise dans ce lit le premier soir, moi qui croyais mourir de

haine et de mépris, j'ai aimé, j'ai gémi de joie sous lui . . . attentive à moi seule, je t'ai oublié jusqu'au matin. (PG. 77).

La Valse des Toréadors is a mellower play. Only the fourth act retains the nightmarish quality of *Ardèle*. The General himself has grown noticeably in stature and acquired a little more dignity than his counterpart in *Ardèle*. He is also languishing in retirement and also tied to a bedridden wife devoured by jealousy. One of his few diversions is dictating his memoirs of his early campaigns to a young secretary, Gaston. Into this unfulfilled but regular existence bursts Ghislaine de Sainte-Euverte, the General's platonic mistress of seventeen years' standing. They danced the Waltz of the Toreadors together that many years ago at a regimental ball and, ever since, have conducted an illicit but chaste affair, mostly from a distance. Unfortunately the fresh young thing with whom the General fell in love is now, alas, a middle-aged and ridiculous old spinister. The reason for her sudden appearance at this juncture is that she has uncovered dramatic proof of an affair between the General's wife Amélie and her doctor. She and the General are free at last! This intrusion provokes a series of mock-serious disturbances, including two attempted suicides. Amélie throws herself onto a disused railway line while Ghislaine jumps out of a window, only to land in a hammock on top of Gaston. This is a fortunate encounter since Ghislaine falls in love with Gaston. General Saint-Pé is ready to do combat to avenge this outrage but the parish priest arrives out of the blue with the news that Gaston is the General's son by a former mistress. The General is finally prevailed upon to overcome his indignation and consent to their marriage. Relative peace returns to his household, and the General consoles himself by slipping an arm around the new maid and inviting her for a little walk in the garden.

Despite the many farcical comings and goings in *La Valse des Toréadors*, the real centre of interest is the death of a human relationship. This is clear in the fourth act which has a stark, nightmarish quality out of keeping with the rest of the play. It is a long, uninterrupted confrontation between the General and Amélie, in her bedroom, full of bitter mutual recriminations at the loss of love and the fading of desire. It ends in a grotesque *danse macabre*, a mockery of the Waltz of the Toreadors, with Amélie taunting her husband:

Viens danser avec ton vieux squelette, avec ta vieille maladie chronique. Viens danser avec ton remords. Viens danser avec ton amour. (PG. 182)

Doctor Bonfont sums up the moral of the play:

Il ne faut jamais comprendre son ennemi — ni sa femme . . . Il ne faut jamais comprendre personne, d'ailleurs, ou on en meurt. (PG. 208)

As the General and the new maid slip out into the garden at the end of the play Anouilh describes them as a "couple dérisoire". Nonetheless, there are moments when the General, this "vieux petit garçon sans grandes exigences" (PG. 210), can excite genuine pathos and sympathy. The play ends on a final note of sad, lucid resignation to life.

La Répétition is a quite different type of play. There are no moments of farcical humour and only the Countess's lover, Villebosse, is an outright caricature. *La Répétition* is, in a sense, two plays in one. As its title suggests, it is a play about rehearsing a play. A group of aristocratic amateurs, under the direction of Count Tigre, are rehearsing Marivaux's *La Double Inconstance*, which they intend to perform at a forthcoming dinner party for the amusement of their high society friends. The rehearsal is taking place in an eighteenth-century château and the characters naturally spend their time in period costumes. Moreover, *La Répétition* itself is so admirably written that it is sometimes difficult to spot the transition from Anouilh to Marivaux. To complicate matters still further, Tigre prides himself on having cast the Marivaux play to correspond to the roles he, his wife and friends play in real life:

Quand j'ai distribué la pièce, j'ai très bien su ce que je faisais. (PB. 390)

La Double Inconstance is the story of a shepherdess, Sylvia, who is in love with a fellow peasant, Arlequin, and is also desired by a more noble suitor, the Prince, whose courtiers conspire to make Arlequin forget Sylvia and allow their master to win her in the end. Tigre plays the Prince, not only because he is prince of his own little closed society but also because he intends to use the rehearsal to seduce Lucile, a young governess who is looking after a party of orphans in a wing of the château and who of course is playing Sylvia. His wife Éliante and his mistress Hortensia, for whom life is a carefully maintained façade of elegance and good manners, find this liaison undignified and offensive. To destroy it they enlist the aid of Tigre's friend, Héro, who bears Tigre an old grudge. They lure Tigre away with a fake urgent telegram and, during his absence, Héro manages to seduce Lucile. She is overcome by shame and remorse and leaves Tigre forever.

The main theme and situation of this play are familiar from *Le Rendez-vous de Senlis*: a middle-aged married man who has experienced the disillusioning effects of time and life on love falls in love with a young innocent girl and is offered a second chance. The difference is that whereas *Le Rendez-vous de Senlis* ended happily if inconclusively, there is now no reprieve possible. The subtitle of *La Répétition* is *Love punished*.

The main theme of these years is still the constant central conflict between reality and the ideal. The slow but sure attrition of living degrades all our hopes and dreams, just as those who chose suicide had feared. This defeat may come from without as in the case of Lucile and Tigre. But it may equally come from within as in Julien's case, and that is a surer sign of the maturing of Anouilh's own vision and his increasingly objective treatment of his own heroes.

It is an easy step from this pessimistic vision to seeing Anouilh's portrayal of life as a *farce grinçante* as the wounded idealist's revenge and the expression of an anger "too savage, intense and unforgiving to be accommodated within the limits of comedy".[1] This purely negative view is only half the story. As in *L'Invitation au château*, the dramatic form both expresses a bleak vision of life and offers an antidote to it. Before defining what that is we must look at the constituent parts of Anouilh's new style.

In *L'Invitation au château* Anouilh borrowed from the resources of traditional comic drama and, in so doing, opened up a long, historical perspective on his craft. This process is continued and amplified here. At first sight Anouilh's borrowings in these plays seem as mixed as the plays themselves. His use of farce, by his own admission, belongs to the purest Molieresque tradition and Molière's influence is everywhere apparent in these plays.[2] *La Valse des Toréadors* is structured around one character, the General Saint-Pé, like a Molière character comedy, while *Colombe* is strongly reminiscent of *L'École des Femmes* and, at times, of *Le Misanthrope*. The spirit of Marivaux hovers over *La Répétition*. But there are also more modern influences at work. That of Strindberg is felt in Anouilh's preoccupation with the couple. Strindberg's *Danse macabre* was produced several times in Paris during the forties and Roland Laudenbach, who accompanied Anouilh to one of these productions, confirms the importance which Anouilh himself attaches to Strindberg's influence on his work.[3] Strindberg's battle of the sexes is most obvious in *La Valse des Toréadors*. It can also be seen in the battle of wits between Tigre and Éliane in *La Répétition* and in the conflict between male rigour and female facility in *Col-*

[1] S. John, 'Obsession and Technique in the Plays of Jean Anouilh', *French Studies*, April 1957, p. 113.

[2] *Paris-Presse*, Oct. 14th 1951. On Molière and Anouilh, cf. W. D. Howarth, *Molière: Stage and Study*, pp. 273–288.

[3] A. Swerling, *Strindberg's Impact in France: 1920–1960*, p. 166.

ombe. Another important influence from the forties was Roger Vitrac, to whom *La Valse des Toréadors* is dedicated. Anouilh saw Vitrac's surrealist drama *Victor ou les enfants au pouvoir* in 1947 and was so impressed by this "remarkable production" that he described it as his second revelation in the theatre, after Giraudoux's *Siegfried* in the thirties. Vitrac's play is about a prodigiously precocious nine-year-old and the disruption he causes within the family. Anouilh confessed to having plagiarized it in *Ardèle* and felt that he had come closest to Vitrac's style of theatre in *Ardèle* and *La Valse des Toréadors*. Anouilh enjoyed a long friendship with Vitrac and there is no doubt that Vitrac's attempt to portray human beings in their "absurdité intégrale" was a strong corroborative influence on Anouilh's own thinking.[1] Last but not least among modern influences is the silent cinema of Charlie Chaplin, Max Sennet and Max Linder. Anouilh makes specific reference to this in relation to *La Valse des Toréadors*, where he praises Claude Sainval, who played the General, for restoring to the theatre a style of poetic acting lost since the eclipse of the silent classics.[2]

It is neither possible nor desirable to list all the borrowings and influences evident in these plays. What is of interest is not their diversity but their common origins. Molière through farce and Marivaux through the *Commedia dell'Arte* hark back to more ancient comic sources. Even the Strindbergian battle of the sexes goes back, through Molière and Marivaux, to ultimately mythological sources. Vitrac's surrealist comedy is, in Anouilh's opinion, not so much an innovation as a "retour à la vieille source française des fabliaux et de Molière."[3] Equally, the pantomine and slapstick comedy of the silent classics belongs to the same ancient and everlasting comic traditions. In other words, Anouilh is borrowing from different stages and manifestations of an old and constant stream of comic inspiration in order to recreate "un très ancien style de jeu qui remonte aux Atellanes, passe par la Commedia dell'Arte, les Tréteaux du Pont-Neuf pour aboutir à l'Illustre Théâtre et, j'en suis persuadé, à la façon de jouer du patron du théâtre français" (i.e. Molière).[4] The result is a conglomerate form made up of elements, as far as it is possible to separate them, from the *drame*, melodrama, farce, vaudeville, Commedia dell'Arte, circus, Guignol,

[1] Cf. Anouilh on Vitrac in *Le Figaro Littéraire*, Oct. 6th 1962, *Le Monde*, Oct. 4th 1962 and Vandromme, op. cit., pp. 171–173.

[2] *Le Figaro*, Jan 23rd 1952.

[3] *Le Figaro Littéraire*, loc. cit.

[4] Anouilh in the programme note for a revival of *La Valse des Toréadors* in *L'Avant-Scène*, May 15th 1974.

pantomine and slapstick comedy. This form in turn allows Anouilh to transpose a dark, pessimistic vision of life into comic terms by subjecting it, in his own words, to a "procédé vaudevillesque et caricatural"[1].

This treatment was greatly misunderstood at the time, so much so that *La Valse des Toréadors*, in which it is most developed, was a flop. Criticism was so widespread and severe that Anouilh, by nature a shy, retiring writer not given to manifestos, was driven to write a defence of the play, *La Valse des Toréadors: que voilà une bonne pièce!*[2] This is a valuable document since it is one of the few in which Anouilh explains the intentions behind his techniques. He deals in it with two important aspects or effects of the "procédé vaudevillesque et caricatural". The first of these concerns the architecture of the plays. Defending his own practice, he declares:

> Voilà enfin un dramaturge qui comprend que le théâtre est avant tout un libre jeu de l'esprit, que la vraisemblance, une intrigue soigneusement menée, des entrées et des sorties habilement agencées ne sont rien.[3]

The plays bear out this conviction in a manner which recalls *Le Voyageur sans bagage*, where, by manipulating levels of impression, Anouilh had appeared unwilling to shoulder the traditional burden of writing a play. Here expositions are obvious and forthright. In *Ardèle* and *La Valse des Toréadors* we are into the heart of the matter in minutes. Even in *La Répétition* where the exposition is more leisurely, no attempt is made to disguise it as anything other than the exposition. *Dénouements* are as obvious and peremptory as the expositions. In *Ardèle* a situation which could last indefinitely is brought to a sudden climax by the lovers' suicide. Then, Anouilh's point made, it is abandoned. In *La Valse des Toréadors* the situation is resolved by a glaringly artificial recognition device borrowed from melodrama, when Gaston is revealed to be the General's son.

It is particularly appropriate in the farces that sudden entrances and exits, surprise twists in the plot, outrageous coincidences and bouts of knockabout chaos remove any semblance of careful construction or probability. Rapid transitions in mood and tone, from comic to serious, from outright farce to pathos also create a generally unsettled and unfinished impression in all the plays of this period, which seem at times to belong more to the unpredictable and troubling realms of dreams than to the solid world of the well-made play. We have already seen the nightmarish qualities of *Ardèle* and

[1] *Le Figaro*, loc. cit.
[2] ibid.
[3] ibid.

the fourth act of *La Valse des Toréadors*. Anouilh was taken to task for just such breaks in tone, general disunity and lack of tightness in construction. His answer came in reply to similar criticisms of one of Roger Vitrac's plays:

La pièce coule nonchalamment, on ne sait trop d'où elle vient ni où elle va. Et après? Laissez les lois de l'architecture aux spécialistes du bâtiment, le théâtre est un jeu de l'esprit, et l'esprit peut très bien faire son miel en butinant de détail en détail, comme l'abeille.[1]

The same perplexity and criticism greeted the other major aspect of Anouilh's vaudevillesque and caricatural treatment—his use of caricature. Caricaturization is by no means new to Anouilh. His plays abound in caricatures from the earliest times. But in this period he uses caricature in a new way and on a new scale. In *Le Rendez-vous de Senlis* he had been hesitant about putting outright caricatures in main roles. Now he creates principal characters who, like the General in *La Valse des Toréadors*, are "à la fois une marionnette . . . et un personnage humain".[2]

The plays still teem with minor characters who are outright caricatures, of course. Such are all the highly entertaining denizens of the backstage world in *Colombe*. Creations such as Villardieu in *Ardèle* and Villebosse in *La Répétition* are also on the lowest rung of caricature. They are typified by repetitive phrases and moments of self-oblivious, mechanistic behaviour. But, for the first time, the main characters or heroes also share these traits. In *Colombe*, Julien's sense of honour has become an *idée fixe*, which threatens to possess his faculties and reduce him to the mechanistic behaviour of the stereotype. There are moments when he seems already possessed.[3] But Julien is still a relatively realistic creation compared to the Generals who are the most ambitious and successful achievements in blending character and caricature. They rush about at times behaving incoherently and ridiculously like clowns or puppets. But there are also moments when they speak with disconcertingly human voices of their regrets, disappointments and failures in life, with an emotional realism and lucidity we do not expect from caricatures. This procedure can obviously be offputting at first. Indeed, it is calculated to have a certain shock value. Anouilh was predictably taken to task by the critics for inconsistency and lack of cohesion. Yet, after all, twentieth-century psychologists have long since discredited the idea that human personality is a fixed and easily defin-

[1] *Opéra*, March 7th 1951.
[2] *Le Figaro*, loc. cit.
[3] PB. 180.

able thing. In that respect Anouilh is hardly breaking new ground. Indeed, it could be argued that this fusion of character and caricature has more psychological truth and is closer to real life than other, apparently more realistic modes of character drawing. The whole truth is that we do behave illogically and inconsistently at times and sensibly and reasonably at other times.

It is significant that Anouilh defines realism in the theatre as "l'image encore aplatie, si c'est possible, de l'image déjà terriblement conventionnelle que les hommes se font de leur condition".[1] His blend of realistic characterization and caricature is an attempt to get behind the two-dimensional, flattened image of realism and paint man in the round, in all his *absurdité intégrale*. The realistic illusion, in Anouilh's view, is part of "l'effort des hommes pour faire autour d'eux la réalité sublime ou raisonnable".[2] The truth of the matter is that "nous vivons dans un univers bouffon et nous n'osons pas le voir".[3] By depicting life as a *farce grinçante* and showing us that "nous sommes drôles, même quand nous croyons être nobles ou pathétiques",[4] Anouilh is destroying the flattering illusions of realism and confronting us with the grim but farcical truth.

The positive side of this farcical transposition of life lies in the two aspects of Anouilh's "procédé vaudevillesque et caricatural" discussed above. This process is an attack on the mature, adult, intellectual and rational pleasures associated with the drama: following the logical development of the plot, appreciating careful preparation of events and perceiving the harmonies, symmetries and coherence of the overall dramatic construction. In place of these we find a more forthright and piecemeal presentation of action and events. This is an attempt to deflect attention away from the coherent whole and onto its constituent parts. Significantly, this is also the child's perception of the world. As the nineteenth-century critic Taine remarked:

> Pesez ce mot, l'ensemble; selon qu'on y songe ou non, on entre dans la maturité ou l'on reste dans l'enfance.[5]

Anouilh's vaudevillesque and caricatural treatment invites us to remain in childhood and see the absurdity of the world through the child's eyes. His use of caricature permits an equally forthright,

[1] Vandromme, op. cit., p. 171.
[2] ibid.
[3] Anouilh commenting on Vitrac's characterization in *Le Figaro Littéraire*, loc. cit.
[4] ibid.
[5] Quoted in Lucas, *Tragedy: Serious Drama in relation to Aristotle's Poetics*, p. 92.

immediate presentation of character, with all the colourful exaggeration and oversimplification we associate with the child's view of things. It also helps present people, immediately and individually, without reference to their complex social functions and interrelations, in other words without reference to the 'whole'. In one sense, then, these plays have left behind the values of a childlike vision of the world which dominated earlier plays. But, in another way, the childlike vision is still there—in the dramatic form and style of the plays themselves. It is this appeal to the child in us which constitutes the positive side of Anouilh's farcical transposition of human absurdity. This absurdity can be either tragic or comic depending on how we view it. Seeing it through the naive and simple eyes of the child renders it laughable and its depiction harmless. Anouilh rejected criticisms that *La Valse des Toréadors* was objectionable and horrifying. The misunderstanding arose because critics had not entered into the proper—childish—spirit of the game. Whereas he was playing marbles, they had wanted to play mummies and daddies! He described the play as:

> un scénario de Max Sennet ou de Feydeau, à travers la trame duquel des sentiments *vrais*, parfois tragiques, mais rendus inoffensifs et *propres au jeu de l'esprit* par la déformation caricaturale, nous sont offerts. A nous de jouer avec eux. Le jeu et les couleurs sont sans danger, l'esprit est foncièrement sain, la conclusion éminemment morale . . . et l'on rit d'un bout à l'autre, même et surtout aux moments où l'on devrait pleurer.[1]

All of this is bravely confident but it conceals a fundamental doubt. The very fact that Anouilh was driven to write a defence of *La Valse des Toréadors* at all shows that not everybody found the game as amusing or harmless as he had hoped. *La Valse des Toréadors*, as Anouilh admits elsewhere, "côtoie quelquefois les horreurs de Strindberg".[2] The dramatist may do his best to render this content harmless but there is always another participant in the theatrical game upon whom the game's success or failure ultimately depends. Anouilh has from the adoption of a ludic approach in *Le Voyageur sans bagage* repeatedly asked for a willing and active contribution from us, his audience. If this period is to be one of renewal for Anouilh personally, then it must also be one for his public. He has tried to re-create the conditions of a childlike vision of life in the form of the plays, but he cannot make us accept it. That depends on our finding within ourselves, in an age characterized by the rediscovery of the Absurd and dominated, in Anouilh's view, by

[1] *Le Figaro*, loc. cit.
[2] *L'Avant-Scène*, loc. cit.

"les philosophes ennuyeux du désespoir qui découvrent périodiquement et un peu ingénument l'horreur de la condition humaine",[1] the kind of childlike simplicity which has sustained a naive comic tradition from time immemorial.

Despite Anouilh's confidence in defence of *La Valse des Toréadors*, he betrays his awareness of this problem. One play in particular, *La Répétition*, deals with just this question—the possibility of a modern twentieth-century audience accepting a tradition seemingly foreign to its own outlook. *La Répétition* appears superficially to be the odd one out among the plays of this period but, like *Antigone* before it, it in fact dramatizes a debate or problem central to Anouilh's whole artistic endeavour at the time.

The central theme of *La Répétition* is renewal and the play has clear mythological overtones. At its heart, enshrined in *La Double Inconstance*, is a pastoral idyll of the love of a Prince for a shepherdess, which belongs to an old comic tradition with its roots in the symbolic re-enactment of cycles of renewal and regrowth, and the replacement of an old order by a new.[2] Anouilh recognizes this dimension and takes advantage of it. Tigre and Éliane have a sterile, childless marriage. They tolerate each other's extramarital relationships as long as these do not infringe the elegant but hypocritical standards by which they live. Lucile is not only pure, young and innocent in herself, she is also, significantly, associated with children. She represents fertility and renewal: the intrusion of a fresh, youthful, genuine and uncompromising emotion into a graceful but sterile society. For Tigre she represents a second chance to recover the lost innocence of youth and live life again. In the event this renewal does not take place because adult society closes ranks to resist and prevent it.

There are in fact two societies in *La Répétition*. One is a modern, urbane, theatre-going society of which Anouilh paints an unattractive picture. It is a hermetic, self-preoccupied élite which uses the theatre to attenuate the boredom of a superficial, constricting and sterile lifestyle. The other society is that of the eighteenth century, present through the kind of theatre it created and enjoyed. From the implicit contrast between them emerges Anouilh's diagnosis of the contemporary *mal du siècle*.

The twentieth century prides itself on being a more democratic age than the eighteenth. It is only such a modern democratic regard

[1] Vandromme op. cit., p. 143.

[2] Cf. Steinberg and Mowshowitz, '*La Répétition* par Jean Anouilh: une nouvelle lecture', *Études françaises*, IX, no. 2, 1973.

for the fundamental human rights and dignity of the individual that explains and justifies Tigre's striking analysis of *La Double Inconstance* as "proprement l'histoire élégante et gracieuse d'un crime" (PB. 375). The crime Tigre has in mind is that the Prince's courtiers should conspire to make both Arlequin and Sylvia forget their own genuine love and fall in love with others. Yet it is obvious from various examples of their own snobbery and prejudice that the society of which Tigre is prince is every bit as élitist and hierarchical as its eighteenth-century counterpart. Moreover, in one important respect, modern sophisticated society is more inflexible than it was in the eighteenth century. Eighteenth-century society could at least permit its Princes and commoners to marry in the theatre whereas the nominally more democratic twentieth century will not. It clearly did not experience the same unease and distaste at a naive idyllic tradition which modern sophisticated society does in the person of Éliane, who finds her husband's love for Lucile graceless and ridiculous. The modern world has lost the unself-conscious simplicity necessary to indulge the idyll.

Anouilh uses theatre-in-the-theatre to illustrate this difference in the sensibilities of the two centuries. The mock *dénouement* of *La Double Inconstance* at the end of Act II, with all the characters taking a bow in period costume, is obviously a theatrical effect. In these first two acts Tigre has used his role as the Prince to court and win Lucile-Sylvia. The curtain-call at the end of Act II celebrates his success. But this is not the real end of a real play for a modern audience, and the remaining three acts are devoted to destroying Tigre's success. If *La Double Inconstance* is to be replayed at all it must be played not as the "conte de fées" (PB. 452) of the Prince and Sylvia, but as the tragedy of Sylvia and Arlequin. As Tigre himself has already indicated, it is the crime and the tragedy, not the idyll, which impresses itself upon the contemporary mind.

Adult sophistication, in the person of Éliane, is unable or unwilling to countenance the innocent simplicity of a naive, comic tradition. She has refused the challenge to her sensibilities offered by a fairytale romance which offends her self-conscious elegance and sophistication. By maintaining her lucidity and exercising her intelligence she destroys the love of Tigre and Lucile. In one sense she has emerged triumphant but, in another more important respect, she has lost. She is left, with her sterile intelligence, in a hard-hearted and anti-sentimental adult world which has not been regenerated by contact with the comic tradition.

Yet the fate of those involved in the idyll is hardly any better. Tigre, previously a paragon of detached, intelligent living, becomes emotionally involved in the theatrical game when he decides to use his role in *La Double Inconstance* as the vehicle for a real emotion. Consequently, he loses his lucidity and his control over the illusion he is attempting to manipulate. His position is fraught with ironies. We have seen how he is easily fooled by Éliane's patently theatrical stratagem of the false telegram. He seems, in fact, unaware of the full implications of his own analysis of the Marivaux play as the story of a crime. He overlooks the fact that, since Lucile has never loved before, there is no equivalent of Arlequin in her life. By falling in love with her Tigre is therefore taking on two roles, that of Prince and also that of Arlequin. It follows logically that if he is to succeed as Prince, he must fail as Arlequin. The outcome of the real play only vindicates his initial insight into *La Double Inconstance*.

Héro also suffers from an overemotional involvement in the theatrical game. He agrees to Éliane's plan because he bears Tigre an old grudge. Many years before, Tigre persuaded him not to marry the young and innocent Évangéline with whom he was very much in love. Évangéline subsequently made an unhappy marriage and died of a broken heart. Having given up his own chance of true love, Héro resents Tigre finding it at this late stage. But for Héro, seducing Lucile and destroying Tigre's second chance is like losing Évangéline all over again. Shortly afterwards he commits virtual suicide by provoking a duel with the expert marksman Villebosse.

The fates of Tigre and Héro, and of Lucile who is caught between them, illustrate the dangers of over-involvement. For them the theatrical game has not proved harmless and the "sentiments vrais, parfois tragiques" it contains have not been held in check. The final solution to successful participation must then be a compromise, perhaps even a paradox. We must make some effort to regenerate within our adult and rational selves the childlike vision and simplicity of mind of that age-old comic inspiration on which the theatrical game of these years is based. This is the prime condition on which what is comic in the revelation of man's *absurdité intégrale* outweighs the horror. It is our laughter which makes the play both a harmless and a successful "jeu de l'esprit". At the same time we must also retain some degree of adult lucidity and detachment. Otherwise we risk an overemotional involvement as a result of which the game ceases to be a game and we start to play in earnest. In that case the real and tragic emotions involved become harmful and destructive once more.

The present chapter is a period of reassessment and re-evaluation which consolidates that "nouvelle voie pour mon théâtre" Anouilh was seeking in 1946 and ushers in a new phase in his evolution. The various contributing influences which bear upon the period are part of his attempt to forge a new style and form. This, as always, is a mixture of old and new. This chapter has most affinities with Chapter Two. There Anouilh first defined his ludic view of the theatre and there too he dipped into the stock-in-trade of theatrical clichés and conventions. In that instance he was using these devices and techniques for their own sake, to underline the artificial and conventionalized nature of the dramatic process. Here his view of the theatre as a game of the intellect and his borrowings from theatrical tradition take on a new importance, derived from Anouilh's long, historical view of the theatre's function and the worth of the dramatist's *métier*.

In this respect the indications in *L'Invitation au château* of what direction Anouilh's new way would take are confirmed. Playing for fun is a way of playing in earnest. The theatrical game has offered mankind a means of transposing tragic truths about himself into comic and conventionalized images from time immemorial. By laughing at these truths, we render them harmless and, in a sense, exorcise them. Now that life is something to be lived, not rejected, it is the theatre's function to help reconcile us to them. As Horace said in *L'Invitation au château*, we cannot remedy the absurdity of existence nor alter our ultimate destiny: but we have just time to play the theatrical game before being—to borrow Horace's phrase from *L'Invitation au château*—"quite dead".

This in turn confirms the growing importance attached to accepting and performing one's *métier* from *Antigone* onwards. The prominence of this idea reveals Anouilh's own search for an ethical basis for his activities as a dramatist, in a period of changing values and standards. In this context the influence of Molière in Chapter Five is far from accidental. An implicit comparison with Molière, whom Anouilh regards as the patron saint of French theatre, is part of Anouilh's historical view of his theatre's function:

> il y a une évidence simple qu'on oublie: nous avons fait le même métier.[1]

Anouilh's view of Molière, regardless of its historical accuracy, throws light upon his own view of the theatre's purpose. He defends Molière against the new school of thought which has decided that Molière was a tragedian.[2] He does not deny that there is a tragic substance in Molière. On the contrary, "Molière, dans un moule

[1] *L'Avant-Scène*, loc. cit.
[2] ibid.

de comédie raisonnable, a écrit le théâtre le plus noir de la littérature de tous les temps."[1] But what Anouilh does contest is that Molière intended us to do anything other than laugh at ourselves. Anouilh's Molière "n'a jamais songé qu'à faire rire".[2] Moreover, to do so, he used that same style, old as the Atellan farces, which Anouilh has sought to re-create in these plays:

> Molière, comédien, devait jouer comme ça. Lui aussi faisait déjà des grimaces et trop de gestes pour les loges qui pinçaient le nez—tandis que le parterre hurlait de rire.[3]

Obviously, the balcony still continued, some three hundred years later, to turn its nose up at *La Valse des Toréadors*. Nonetheless, the challenge of Anouilh's new style remains. In *La Répétition* he shows the hurdles of contemporary sophistication and intellectualism we must surmount to participate in this new version of the theatrical game. But, as always, the initiative must come from us.

[1] Vandromme, op. cit., p. 141.
[2] *L'Avant-Scène*, loc. cit.
[3] ibid.

VI. Heroes and Antiheroes

L'Alouette – Ornifle – Pauvre Bitos – L'Hurluberlu – Becket

"For those who serve the greater cause may make the cause serve them." (Eliot, *Murder in the Cathedral*)

The failure of *La Valse des Toréadors* made a deep impression upon Anouilh. It was the most successful expression of his new style and also the most misunderstood and denigrated. His audiences, particularly his critics, had not absorbed the lesson of *La Répétition*. Speaking some ten years later of the influence of Vitrac's theatre on his own work, Anouilh said:

> Encore aujourd'hui je pense que c'est le théâtre que j'aurais voulu écrire. Je crois m'en être rapproché dans *Ardèle* et *La Valse des Toréadors*. L'accident, l'échec de *La Valse* . . . m'a été fatal. J'ai inconsciemment changé de voie.[1]

Artistic and professional disappointment alone does not account for this change, however. It has already been suggested that Anouilh's personal circumstances were a contributing factor to his mood in the early fifties. Anouilh himself suggests that the composition of *L'Alouette*, the first play of this new group, was to a great extent the result of a change in those circumstances. Recalling the genesis of the play, he defined the creative impulse behind it as "une inexplicable joie".[2] That is indeed what radiates from the subject of the play and its treatment.

His version of the Joan of Arc story is both highly theatrical and strikingly original. The actors come on stage, pick up their props left behind from an earlier production and start discussing how they will re-enact Joan's life and trial. Her English captor, Warwick, wants understandably to proceed immediately to her trial and condemnation, but Bishop Cauchon, who presides over the proceedings, insists that "elle a toute sa vie à jouer avant" (PC. 12). The play is effectively her trial but the initial air of improvisation is maintained by frequent flashbacks in which Joan and the other characters re-enact scenes of her past life. As in the medieval

[1] *Le Monde*, Oct. 4th 1962.
[2] Vandromme, op. cit., p. 219.

theatre—and appropriately enough, given this medieval subject—the stage is used as a single, integrated acting space where scenes can be presented in succession or simultaneously with a minimum of fuss and scenery and a maximum of imagination. It is nominally the place of Joan's trial but serves, as need arises, as Joan's home village of Domrémy, the battlefields on which she fought, the Dauphin's court at Chinon or her prison cell. Characters not directly involved in each episode often remain in the background and Joan's ecclesiastical judges intervene on occasion to question her version of events. The presentation of character is equally theatrical. Given Anouilh's wide historical canvas and the large number of episodic characters, most can only be caricatures to a greater or lesser degree. This works admirably in fact and complements the fragmented, episodic structure. These caricatures are perfectly at home in brief animated vignettes and they spring immediately to life. Even among more important characters there are no naturalistic creations. Anouilh's portrait of Joan is realistic in one sense. There is nothing of the distant, immortalized saint about her. On the contrary, she is an engagingly human and down-to-earth country girl whose plain-spokenness, humour and common sense sometimes confound the theologians around her. Once or twice Anouilh uses her actual words, taken from trial records, but his portrait falls far short of documentary realism.

Joan is a theatrical heroine in another sense also. She conforms to the pattern of behaviour already established by Antigone and typical of the heroic race's rejection of life in Anouilh's plays. She defends her visions and sense of mission tenaciously until she is intimidated by the threat of torture into renouncing them and submitting to the Church. In prison she is visited by Charles and the ladies of his court and her captor Warwick. All of them commend her action and urge her to look forward to life. Joan imagines what she will become:

> Jeanne acceptant tout, Jeanne avec un ventre, Jeanne devenue gourmande. Vous voyez Jeanne fardée, en hennin, empêtrée dans ses robes, s'occupant de son petit chien ou avec un homme à ses trousses, qui sait, Jeanne mariée? (PC. 131)

Like Antigone, she rebels at this prospect of 'happiness', reaffirms her divine mission and goes to her death. *L'Alouette* was one of Anouilh's greatest successes but some voices were raised in a familiar protest: that once again Anouilh had debased a noble subject by subordinating it to his own preoccupations. But his greatest surprise is reserved for the end. Joan is duly condemned and the actors set about constructing her funeral pyre. Just as they have set it alight, in rushes Captain Beaudricourt, who first befriended Joan, and reminds them that they have not acted the Dauphin's coronation scene in Rheims cathedral. The pyre is hastily dismantled. An organ sounds, bells peal and the play ends with a tableau of Joan triumphant, sword in hand and banner waving, in a resplendent tableau of the coronation scene. Anouilh describes this final tableau as the kind of beautiful illustration you might find in a school prize book[1] and his whole treatment of the subject is inspired by this view of history.

As we watch the colourful spectacle of this pageant of schoolbook history, we cannot but be struck by the change in mood from *La Valse des Toréadors* of a year earlier. But Anouilh's joy is not entirely inexplicable. In the article mentioned above he confides that he had just acquired a new home in the village of Montfort-L'Amaury outside Paris and that he was "commençant une nouvelle vie".[2] He married the young actress Nicole Lançon in 1953. It is very much the impression of new life that *L'Alouette* makes after the gathering darkness of *La Valse des Toréadors*.

The new period ushered in by *L'Alouette* covers the rest of Anouilh's writing in the fifties. *La Grotte*, written in 1960, is a pivotal work like *L'Invitation au château* and marks another reappraisal by Anouilh of his practice. Like *L'Invitation au château*, it will be treated separately. The last play of this present group is then Anouilh's other major historical work, *Becket*, on the life and death of Thomas à Becket, Archbishop of Canterbury, who was martyred in 1170. The presentation of history here is just as imaginative and theatrical as in *L'Alouette*. It would be more accurate to say cinematic and *Becket* was in fact turned into a successful film in the sixties. The play begins with Henry II of England coming to Canterbury to do penance at the tomb of an already martyred Archbishop. The whole of the action subsequently is recalled in a single uninterrupted flashback, taking place in the King's mind as he remembers the events of their relationship from close friendship through estrangement to death.

Again the stage serves, with great ingenuity and economy of staging, as a variety of locales and the action ranges widely and swiftly, with all the freedom of the cinema, from Canterbury to France to Rome and back to Canterbury. The presentation of history is as vivid and colourful as in *L'Alouette* and the stage is peopled by

[1] PC. 139
[2] Vandromme, op. cit., p. 221.

a similarly large *dramatis personae* of broadly drawn episodic characters. There is some compression of events for dramatic ends, but otherwise the story is accurate in outline and many details. This is not to say, however, that Anouilh's main concern is historical authenticity. His source is Augustin Thierry's *Histoire de la conquête de l'Angleterre par les Normands* published in 1825. It suits Anouilh's own purposes in being a somewhat colourful, romantic view of events, but it has been largely superseded by modern scholarship. It contains two quite incorrect assumptions about Becket's origins which Anouilh has taken over and used in the play: that Becket was illegitimate and a Saxon. Anouilh had already used the situation in *L'Alouette*, with an English army occupying French soil, to create echoes of the German Occupation and the Liberation. Becket's Saxon origins give a racial dimension to his opposition to the King and allow Anouilh to introduce similar issues, such as collaboration and resistance. But he was unrepentant:

> Je n'ai pas été chercher dans les livres qui était vraiment Henri II — ni même Becket. J'ai fait le roi dont j'avais besoin et le Becket ambigu dont j'avais besoin.[1]

This is where Anouilh's real interest lies, in the relationship of these two men; and the play's major theme is the tragic failure of a friendship:

> What struck me was Becket saying to Henry: "Now I am Archbishop I can't continue to be your friend."[2]

In keeping with the theme, the characterization of Henry and Becket is deeper and more elaborate. Becket is a somewhat remote figure. His motto is: "Bien faire ce que j'ai à faire" (PC. 196).

As Henry's friend and Chancellor of England, he is a good companion and defends the King's interests skilfully and well. But when Henry appoints him Archbishop against his wishes he accepts the consequences of his new position, applies his morality to it and opposes the King's attempts to curb the power and privileges of the Church. Henry is as spontaneous and human as Becket is remote. He shows a deep, genuine affection for the older, wiser man and critics were quick to note the homosexual undertones in the relationship. Henry's subsequent struggle with Becket is conducted on two levels. On one level he is pursuing the implementation of his own policies, aimed ultimately at curbing the power of Rome: but

[1] ibid, p. 240.
[2] *Radio Times*, July 14th 1977.

on another he is motivated by all the bitter resentment of unrequited love.

Between these two *pièces costumées*, lie three other major works.[1] Closest to them in form is the semi-historical *Pauvre Bitos*. This is the story of Bitos, son of a washerwoman, who, through hard work and study, has achieved the position of a deputy public prosecutor. When he is appointed to his home town, his former school friends invite him to a *dîner de têtes*, a dinner party at which the guests disguise themselves, from the neck upwards, as historical figures. There is an ulterior motive behind the invitation, however. Bitos's school friends are all aristocrats and wealthy industrialists and their real purpose is to antagonize and humiliate him for his prowess at school, and his present left-wing convictions. In these and in his application of justice Bitos is as zealous as he is rigid. Maxime, host of the dinner party, describes to an early arrival how, rather than show leniency, Bitos ordered the execution of a boyhood friend for collaboration and then went out and bought the victim's little daughter an expensive doll. Maxime's choice of historical period is ominous: the French Revolution. He has asked Bitos to come as Robespierre.

As soon as discussion begins at the dinner table it is clear that the antipathies of Revolutionary France are still very much alive today. Bitos's defence of Robespierre and the Revolution becomes a defence of his own left-wing ideals and the excesses of the *épuration*. This parallel is made even clearer when the gendarme Merda arrives and 'shoots' Bitos, just as the real Merda wounded Robespierre while arresting him in 1794. Bitos faints with fright at this cruel practical joke and a long dream sequence follows in which we return to Revolutionary France. This traces the career of Robespierre but simultaneously it elucidates the development of Bitos's own mind. It amounts to an unattractive portrait of a left-wing idealist. Left-wing critics were suitably incensed. Here is Anouilh's own recollection of the first night:

> The première of Bitos I shall never forget. During the intermission a left-wing critic tried to organize a riot in the lobby. I was jeered at the final curtain and threatened on all sides when I left the theatre. The mob banged

[1] Two shorter plays from this period have also been included in the collected works: *L'Orchestre* (1957) and *La Foire d'empoigne* (1958). The former recalls *La Sauvage*. It features an unmistakably Tardelike café orchestra and the main theme is the contrast between the façade of the performers' stage life and the realities of their backstage lives. The latter is a political farce dealing with The Hundred Days of Napoleon's brief return to power in 1815. It chronicles the disillusionment of an enthusiastic young idealist, D'Anouville, at the hands of his wiser elders.

on the roof of my car as I drove off. I was frightened but thrilled. I had a moment of pride in my work.[1]

Pauvre Bitos is the most obviously politicized of Anouilh's plays up to that date and yet it is not a political play in any party or ideological sense. Anouilh himself insists that "ce n'est absolument pas une pièce politique".[2] Anouilh aims his blows right across the political spectrum from left to right. If Bitos is unsympathetic, so are his aristocratic tormentors. Anouilh's real target is contemporary French society; his real interest is human nature in one of its manifestations—man as a political animal. Bitos is to some extent a victim of his own background, upbringing and complexes and it is possible to feel sorry for him. The "poor Bitos" in the title is meant in this sense. He is in fact saved from final humiliation by one of the guests, Victoire, who feels some sympathy for him. He leaves but with a final threat that, if he can, he will have his revenge one day.

There are several moments of humour in *Pauvre Bitos*. Bitos splits the seat of his trousers in true vaudeville fashion and his struggle with an unruly umbrella is pure pantomine. Even so, we have left the spirit of *L'Alouette* far behind. There is relatively more comedy in the two remaining plays which make clear Anouilh's continuing debt to Molière. *Ornifle* is Anouilh's version of Molière's *Don Juan*. Count Ornifle de Saint-Oignon is, after Tigre, Anouilh's second talented aristocrat. In his youth he was one of the most promising poets of his generation but now divides his time between writing suggestive lyrics for nude reviews and seducing aspiring young actresses. The reason for his conversion is that Ornifle very soon realized the futility of pursuing the unattainable ideal of artistic perfection and decided that henceforth life must be played at but not taken seriously. Yet Ornifle is in his own strange way a man of principle. He pursues his pleasures sometimes against his own instincts and maintains his facile approach to life with a lucid, even grim, determination which suggests his great inner unhappiness and makes him a sympathetic character. He threatens to become less so when he responds to a natural coquettishness in his future daughter-in-law Marguerite and decides, on principle, to seduce her. She is fiancée to his illegitimate son Fabrice, who, returning to kill his unsuspecting father with an empty revolver, only succeeds in provoking a heart attack. Fabrice, a medical student, diagnoses Bishop's disease. This diagnosis is dismissed by two eminent prac-

[1] *International Herald Tribune*, Sept. 18th 1970.
[2] *Les Nouvelles Littéraires*, Feb. 5th 1959.

titioners but Ornifle sees in it an excellent subterfuge for winning his way into Marguerite's affections. But fate strikes before Ornifle can become odious. While going to meet another of his little actresses he collapses and dies. The diagnosis? Bishop's disease.

There are some extremely funny moments in *Ornifle*. The first act for example builds up to a marvellous comic climax with Ornifle composing, almost simultaneously, a Christmas carol for the neighbourhood orphanage and a suggestive ditty for a new review, while posing outrageously for a bevy of photographers. The two doctors who examine Ornifle are complete caricatures, lifted straight out of *Le Malade Imaginaire*. Don Juan's companion Sganarelle has provided two excellent comedy roles. One is Machetu, ex black marketeer, self-made man and theatrical impresario. He agonizes comically over his lack of social graces and the aristocratic Ornifle scores easy points off him. The other is Ornifle's devoted spinster secretary and self-appointed conscience, Mademoiselle Supo. Another *vieille fille* in the Ghislaine de Sainte Euverte mould, she has idolized the master for years of frustrated, repressed desire. Yet one comes away from the play feeling, as with Ornifle himself, that beneath all the outrageous clowning there lies the despair of the disappointed idealist.

L'Hurluberlu completes the trilogy of plays featuring a retired General. There is a good deal of farce in this play also but none of the nightmarishness of its two predecessors in Chapter Five. The General has again grown noticeably in stature. He is as ineffectual and blustering as his counterparts but the caricature is much gentler and he never becomes grotesque. In one important respect he has more affinity with Joan and Becket than with the earlier generals. He has never really resigned himself to life's disappointments:

Il y a un demi-siècle que j'ai de la peine. Cela commence à devenir long. Petit garçon, j'avais vu cela tout autrement. Je ne m'en suis pas remis. (NPG. 38)

Ludovic was France's youngest general on his appointment and, only twenty-six days later, was the youngest to be forcibly retired and jailed for plotting against the régime. But he is an inveterate conspirator and has found another cause to occupy his premature retirement.

Soudain, un beau matin, et par hasard . . . je découvre l'existence des vers. J'étais sauvé . . . Je me suis aperçu que si cela ne tournait plus rond en France, et depuis longtemps, c'est qu'il y avait des vers dans le fruit. Tout était clair enfin: la France était véreuse! (NPG. 12, 13)

Ludovic's worm in the apple is the facility of modern life, the self-interest and lack of earnestness and dedication which are eating away at the heart of contemporary France. He is consequently ringleader of a comically ineffectual village conspiracy—an open secret—to rid France of its worms. Ludovic is a quixotic figure, tilting at impossible windmills. There is also something of Molière's misanthrope Alceste in him and the subtitle of this play, *le réactionnaire amoureux*, is a clear reference to *Le Misanthrope ou l'atrabilaire amoureux*.

On the domestic front Ludovic's life is as chaotic as that of his predecessors. He has to cope with his spinster sister's paranoid sexual fantasies while curbing his adolescent daughter's first experiments with the milkman's son. His eldest daughter Sophie is having an affair with a young urbane sophisticate, David Edward Mendigalès, who tries unsuccessfully to introduce the General to the ways of modern morality and the avant-garde theatre. More poignant is the rearguard action he is fighting to save his marriage to a much younger wife, Aglaé, who is finding life increasingly boring and unfulfilling.

Needless to say Ludovic is fighting a losing battle on all fronts. He is floored, literally, in arguments with David Edward and his aggressive, left-wing milkman. His co-conspirators desert him one by one except for the "prodigiously dim" village ironmonger Ledadu. Aglaé is drifting inevitably into the arms of a charming young playboy. Ludovic is not going to change the world nor restore the honour and rigour he finds lacking in France. But even in defeat he retains dignity. Man, he tells his young son, Toto, is both "inconsolable et gai" (NPG. 159). Even though resigned to his part in life's grotesque little *comédie*, he has the courage to laugh at his own absurdity.

This is essentially the same view of life we found in the plays of Chapter Five, and it is interesting that Anouilh should have spoken of "switching tracks" after *La Valse des Toréadors* and not changing direction. There are many continuities in theme and technique between this chapter and the previous one and also a number of advances. The influence of Molière is, if anything, even more apparent here than in Chapter Five. There is the same bold use of caricature as in the previous chapter and an absorbing advance in the technique of blending character and caricature, which we shall see when we look more closely at some of the main characters. There is also a notable expansion in Anouilh's stagecraft, where he has been inspired by the challenge of large historical subjects to produce a fluid and free-ranging technique which enjoys all the freedom of the cinema and of the human imagination itself. Indeed, it is the human imagination we see at work in the historical plays. The action of *Becket* takes place in Henry's mind, and in *L'Alouette* and *Pauvre Bitos* the principle characters dramatize the past as seen through their own imaginations.

As regards themes, there is still the same eternal conflict between the realities of existence and all of humanity's aspirations and ideals. Love in particular seems just as doomed as in Chapter Five. There are no happy marriages in these plays and young love, as in the persons of Fabrice or Marguerite, is ridiculed. Ornifle admits to having loved only one woman—his present wife—but he paints an unflattering picture of the sentiment:

> On joue le petit ballet du désir comme les toutous. Je te sens, tu me sens, je me détourne, je me retourne, je ne veux pas, si! Je veux bien. Et puisque je veux bien c'est que c'est pour la vie . . . Et puis quelqu'un (on ne sait pas qui) soudain, tire la laisse et le toutou qui rêvait d'éternité s'en va, happé . . . (PG. 275)

One noticeable innovation in this period is the politicization of these plays, in the broad sense already explained. Anouilh's feelings about the Liberation have only surfaced in these plays and not as one might expect in those immediately after the war. There are clear references in all these plays to collaboration, resistance and *épuration*. In particular we find several direct, barbed comments on the inhumanity of the French judicial system.

This view of life and love only confirms what we have already seen in Chapter Five. It is all the more surprising then that, in the two *pièces costumées*, Anouilh seems to be returning to the heroic pattern of his earlier theatre. Like Antigone, both Joan and Becket chose death rather than compromise their ideals by living. Indeed, the *pièces costumées* seem to offer an improvement on the earlier pattern of heroic self-sacrifice because, unlike Antigone who died for herself in an absurd world, Joan and Becket have found worthy causes for which to sacrifice themselves. Critics see in *L'Alouette* the return of "the unconquered heroine"[1] and that "pure idealism Anouilh had searched for in earlier plays",[2] and in *Becket*, a return to the clear-cut values of *La Sauvage*, *Eurydice* or *Antigone*.[3] If this is so, then it seriously impairs the unity of this group of plays and its homogeneity as a stage in Anouilh's thought.

The triumph of Joan and Becket in causes greater than themselves

[1] Pronko, op. cit., p. 37.
[2] M. Archer, *Jean Anouilh*, p. 39.
[3] Howarth, *Becket*, p. 33.

is not, however, all that it seems. This will be clearer when we examine their psychology in more detail. In fact, this view of the hero or heroine in a cause provides the underlying unity of the period. All the main characters of these plays are championing some cause or other. For Joan, it is her divine mission to boot the English out of France. For Becket, it is to protect the honour of God and the independence of his Church. In *L'Hurluberlu*, the honour of God is replaced by the honour of France, or at least Ludovic's conception of what that should be. Bitos's cause in life is the relentless pursuit of justice and the implementation of his left-wing ideals. In *Ornifle* values are reversed. Ornifle has long since seen the futility of pursuing all ideals and accepted that life is not worth all the seriousness and effort we devote to it. Paradoxically, he has elevated his own pursuit of facility and playful approach to living to the dignity of a crusade in itself. The unifying image of this period is, then, that of the hero acting in a cause greater than himself. The constant dialectic between idealism and compromise in Anouilh is here stated in terms of the pursuit of honour and rigour versus the pursuit of facility. *L'Alouette* and *Becket* state the main theme, with the hero and heroine triumphant in a cause. *L'Hurluberlu* is an affectionate and sad parody of the theme, ending in the failure of the hero's cause. *Ornifle* takes this failure as its starting point and states the counter-theme: the pursuit of facility. As for *Pauvre Bitos*, it stands at the centre of the group and provides the key—in the psychological development of Bitos—to understanding Anouilh's real intentions and preoccupations at this time.

It is in the historical dream sequence, after he has been 'shot', that we get the deepest and most prolonged insight into Bitos's psychological make-up. The parallel with Robespierre, in particular, is a revealing commentary by Bitos's subconscious mind upon itself. To understand Bitos the man, we must know Bitos the child. Anouilh quotes and endorses Freud: "Un homme sur mille sort de l'enfance".[1]

This dream sequence gives us several glimpses into the childhood of Bitos–Robespierre which reveal the several formative traumas that have made Bitos what he is. Principal among these are the frustrations and humiliations of poverty and social inferiority, compounded by his own natural gracelessness. It was as much for this as for his academic superiority that Bitos was victimized at school by his aristocratic companions. Bitos's intelligence has not compensated for his other disadvantages. He has been denied what he could

[1] *Paris-Match*, June 13th 1959.

not achieve by intelligence alone and both resents and envies the natural grace and social *savoir-faire* which were his aristocratic companions' birthright. His hatred of the Establishment and his taste for violence also stem from other sources. There is a scene in the dream sequence in which Robespierre is punished for insubordination by one of his Jesuit teachers. It is highly significant that the features of this teacher should resemble those of King Louis XVI.[1] There is also a strong hint of sado-masochism in the way the young Robespierre approaches and handles the rods with which he is punished "avec une curiosité effrayée" (PG. 440). Yet another source of his violence, and the origins of his need for power, lie in his general physical inferiority, particularly in his feelings of sexual inadequacy and jealousy. His hatred of Danton stems from this. Danton is a bull of a man who enjoys life with great gusto and revels in his physical pleasures. His fatal mistake is to vaunt his physical and sexual prowess before Robespierre and to underline Robespierre's fastidiousness and abstinence.

The cumulative effect of these traumas has made Bitos the neurotic, paranoid, sadistic personality that he is. They are the springs of an obsessive monomania which shows itself in the kind of mechanistic, involuntary behaviour we associate with the automaton or the stereotype. In Bitos's case, it is a nervous tick whereby he is continually dusting himself and brushing himself clean. In this we see the profound advance Anouilh has made in his technique of blending character and caricature. He has created in Bitos a fully-fledged character, with a complex psychology, which is then stripped down to reveal the workings of an automaton whose responses are dictated by a number of deep-seated, pathological obsessions. Bitos is in fact the puppet of his own complexes.

This is of more than artistic or technical interest. It affects crucially how we interpret Anouilh's apparent return to the idealism of earlier plays. There is a profound ambiguity in Bitos. His nervous tick also indicates an obsessive need to be rid of his sordid past. The same traumas which determined his career as a left-wing magistrate and champion of the people have instilled in him a horror of everything associated with the common people and poverty and a compulsive need to rise above his origins:

> Mais je n'aime personne. Même pas le peuple. Il pue. Il pue comme mon père qui me cognait dessus et comme les amants de ma mère qui ont continué après, quand il est mort. Et j'ai horreur de ce qui pue. (PG. 494)

[1] PG. 437.

In the last analysis Bitos is a hypocrite and a would-be snob. When the industrialist Brassac hints at a lucrative position with his company Bitos shows himself willing to forsake his egalitarian ideals. The people for Bitos remains an abstract idea with no roots in reality. It is an ideal in the name of which he can take revenge on life for what it has denied him and on those over whom he can exert no natural superiority:

Le sentiment de vous faire peur, à tous, est doux aussi. (PG. 495)

Bitos is an extreme and unpleasant case but, in him, more clearly than elsewhere, the psychology of the cause is explored. We see its origins in the formative traumas of childhood and we realize that it is taken up not out of disinterested concern or intellectual convictions, not even out of a genuine love of humanity, but in response to the deepest needs of his own personality:

Pauvre Robespierre qui tue parce qu'il n'a pas réussi à grandir. (PG. 466)

At first sight the characters in this chapter appeared to have found causes greater than themselves. On closer examination that impression is less sure. The ambiguities of Bitos's *cause du peuple* invite another look at *L'Alouette* and *Becket*.

The whole of *L'Alouette* is a trial convened for the very purpose of contesting the authenticity of Joan's claim to be acting in the name of a cause and authority greater than herself. In the event, her moments of inspired common sense are more than a match for her learned interrogators, but her position is nonetheless undermined by a number of ironies implicit in the overall situation. Firstly the idea that God should intervene and take sides in human battles is an Old Testament concept that, despite popular legend, even a French audience cannot, upon reflection, take seriously. If, on principle, we reject Warwick's claim that "Dieu est avec le droit anglais." (PC. 25) then we must equally query Joan's contention that God is with the French. This problem of the partisanship of God is fundamental to the meaning of the play. In *L'Alouette* all sides look to God for support and justify their actions by claiming a cause and an authority greater than themselves. The Dauphin may be cowardly and weak-willed but he has his moments of insight. Introducing Joan to the unfamiliar game of cards, he explains how an ace is more powerful than a King:

L'as, c'est Dieu si tu veux, mais dans chaque camp. (PC. 75)

There are, moreover, as many different interpretations of God and how his interests may best be defended as there are individuals.

In the light of *Pauvre Bitos*, we suspect that these varying interpretations are the product of individual personalities. Joan's prosecutor, the Promoteur, is a caricature of a fanatic. It is not hard to see that his attacks on Joan's claim to divine inspiration are shaped by his own obsessions with witchcraft and sexuality. The sinister Inquisiteur, official representative of the Inquisition and defender of theological orthodoxy, is more interested in heresy than superstition. But he is another obsessional figure and a prototype for Bitos. His attacks on Joan's naive and unsuspecting humanism are motivated not by intellectual and theological convictions but by a morbid hatred of all humanity. The gentle and sensitive Cauchon, the most fair-minded of Joan's judges, has chosen to collaborate with the English for the sake of peace and stability. Again, his interpretation of what is in the Church's best interests is determined by his own quietist nature:

> Nous n'y pouvons rien . . . Nous ne pouvons que jouer nos rôles, chacun le sien, bon ou mauvais, tel qu'il est écrit et à son tour. (PC. 30)

The cause is not something objective, detached and external to which we harness ourselves. It is rather an expression of the deepest springs of the self. We cannot help seeing Joan's claim to be acting in a cause greater than herself in the context of all the other similar claims which surround her and we must judge them all on the same principles.

Joan's claim is further undermined by historical ironies. These are not discussed in the play but they are implicit in the blatantly contrived ending which ensures that her story is "une histoire qui finit bien" (PC. 139) and Anouilh mentions them in his preface to the play. In reality, after her brief period of success, Joan became an embarrassment to her own side. After her death Charles and his court fell back upon "la bonne vieille politique" (PC. 84) and eventual victory over the English was achieved by more orthodox and reasonable means: a combination of battles won, negotiations from strength and calculated compromise. Joan's only real, lasting achievement was the shining example she created and the splendid image captured in the final tableau of *L'Alouette*, which she left to posterity. Even her canonization in 1920 did not establish her claim to a divine mission. It only verified "l'excellence de ses vertus théologales".[1] She remains "une sainte qui est morte dans une

[1] Anouilh in Vandromme, op. cit., p. 236.

histoire politique".[1] The story of Joan of Arc finishes well but it does not support her triumph in a cause greater than herself.

The ironies implicit in *L'Alouette* increase and become explicit in *Becket*. They are in fact built into the flashback structure of the play and inherent in Anouilh's treatment of history. There are, we remember, two deliberate historical inaccuracies in Anouilh's portrait of Becket—his illegitimacy and his Saxon origins. Becket is twice an alien at the Norman court and he feels this keenly:

> moi, je me suis introduit, en trichant, dans la file — double bâtard. (PC. 187)

This sense of alienation has created in him a deep-seated need to belong, to feel himself part of an order or system with which he can legitimately and honourably identify. He is, in Anouilh's analysis, "l'homme d'une époque où les rapports humains—basés sur la fidelité d'un homme à un autre homme—étaient simples".[2] Thus he is happiest in a feudal relationship which confers on him a well-defined role within a fixed, hierarchical system. The successive roles he plays—King's friend, soldier and Chancellor—allow him to "improviser son honneur" (PC. 187), in his own words, and practise his morality of doing well what he has to do.

But Becket is a man with no real honour. Illegitimate and a Saxon collaborator at the Norman court, he is only playing at playing his various roles. The feudal system of which he is a part is an alien one to which he cannot belong wholeheartedly:

> Mon Prince, si tu étais mon vrai prince, si tu étais de ma race, comme tout serait simple. De quelle tendresse je t'aurais entouré, dans un monde en ordre, mon prince. Chacun l'homme d'un homme, de bas en haut, lié par serment et n'avoir plus rien d'autre à se demander, jamais. (PC. 187)

When he is made Archbishop, Becket takes on yet another role and moves from one feudal system with the King at its centre to another fixed medieval system with God at its centre. The crucial difference is that Becket has now found his "true prince", a lord whom a Saxon may serve legitimately and with honour, without "cheating". Henceforth, as the astute Louis of France observes, the honour of God is inseparable from the honour of Thomas Becket:

> Il n'aime rien au monde que l'idée qu'il s'est forgée de son honneur. (PC. 265)

In this lies the profound, inescapable ambiguity of Anouilh's

[1] ibid.
[2] Vandromme, op. cit., p. 239.

Becket. We cannot separate his defence of God's honour from his own long quest since childhood for an honourable role with which he can fully identify. His decision at the end of the play to return from exile in France to Canterbury, despite certain death, is an indication of the morality by which he has always lived:

La seule chose qui soit immorale, mon prince, c'est de ne pas faire ce qu'il faut, quand il le faut. (PC. 208)

His cause and mission are also undermined from without by historical ironies, as was the case with Joan in *L'Alouette*. At the beginning of the play a triumphant Becket, Saint and martyr, speaks from beyond the grave to a penitent King Henry who is preparing to be scourged for his sins at his former Archbishop's tomb. But this is what we would call nowadays a public relations exercise, intended to win favour with his subjects and unite the nation behind him and his policies. In purely political and historical terms it is the King who triumphs in the end. Becket died to defend the integrity of the Church against the encroachment of the State but Henry has manipulated his death to an exactly opposite effect:

L'Angleterre lui devra sa victoire finale sur le chaos . . . (PC. 295)

Becket's legacy, like Joan's, is not a worldly one. The cause for which the hero dies is ultimately himself. His only legacy to men is his own eternal image and example. *L'Alouette* and *Becket* are not then in contradiction with the mood of the rest of this period, and they do not reinstate the pure idealism and clear-cut values of earlier years. Yet the possibility of just such a return is implicit in the debate between rigour and facility which runs through all these plays. Becket, for example, who as King's friend and Chancellor played at life, gives up this facility and begins to play in earnest when he is appointed Archbishop. But the ironies attendant on this conversion mean we cannot accept this selfless devotion to a cause uncritically. Ornifle's comment comes to mind:

Il n'est pas beau à voir, le visage du don de soi. Quel égoïsme indécent. (PG. 261)

Ornifle, like Camus' Don Juan, knows the "terrible amertume de ceux qui ont eu raison".[1] The ambiguous motives of Joan and Becket vindicate his lucid and determined crusade against the inevitable self-deluding egoism of all life's great causes. He feels and reflects the tenor of the times. He shudders at the mention of his own early work:

[1] Camus, 'Le donjuanisme', *Le Mythe de Sisyphe*, p. 104.

Ils ne sont plus de moi ces poèmes. J'ai horreur d'en entendre parler. C'est à l'époque que je les écrivais dans une mansarde de Saint-Michel où je croyais à la lune, qu'il fallait venir me féliciter. (PG. 234)

Times have changed and the artist himself has grown older. This heroic age is long past, a time of youthful enthusiasm and uncritical naivety which could still countenance the earnest pursuit of idealism. The local priest Père Dubaton recalls the delight and expectations in Catholic *milieux* when Ornifle wrote his *Cantata* on the life of Saint Bernadette, and their disappointment that "depuis, le ton a beaucoup changé" (PG. 238). It is difficult not to see this as Anouilh's answer to those who hailed *L'Alouette* as his return in earnest to what Père Dubaton calls "les grands sujets". But to Ornifle these subjects seem futile:

Quand on fera les comptes . . . on s'apercevra que seuls ceux qui ont amusé les hommes leur auront rendu un véritable service sur cette terre. Je ne donne pas cher des réformateurs, ni des prophètes, mais il y aura quelques hommes futiles qu'on révérera à jamais. Eux seuls auront fait oublier la mort. (PG. 241)

The theatre can no longer tackle "les grands sujets" seriously but it can still entertain and that is just as worthwhile a function. To the young David Edward Mendigalès this is anathema. We are the temporary inhabitants of a planet threatened by atomic destruction. We have neither the time nor the right to amuse ourselves and it is the theatre's job to confront us with the stark revelation of the tragic absurdity of life. The General is unconvinced:

bombe atomique ou non, nous avons toujours été des habitants provisoires de cette planète. Cela ne nous empêchait pas de rire de temps en temps. (NPG. 87)

Anouilh has not then revised that view of the theatre stated in Chapter Five. Nor has he abandoned the childlike vision of things. Ludovic wonders if mankind has not taken an enormous step backwards in the search for truth by renouncing poetry and imagination as means of scientific investigation.[1] Anouilh takes up the same point in his preface to *L'Alouette*, which he calls significantly *Mystère de Jeanne* and in which he derides as naive and futile the insistence of modern thinkers in explaining the mysterious.[2] The "mystery" of Joan of Arc defies rational analysis and his imaginative presentation of history in *L'Alouette* bears witness to this conviction. Anouilh sat down to write *L'Alouette* with nothing to hand but his childhood

[1] NPG. 30.
[2] Vandromme, op. cit., p. 235.

memories of the legend.[1] He subsequently turned to the history books but even so, as Ginestier remarks, there is a quality in the play which appeals to the eternal child in us.[2] Joan's triumph in the final schoolbook image of the play is not a vindication of her claim to a divine mission. It is rather an admission that it belongs to the realms of childhood and the imagination. It must inevitably be challenged in an adult, rational, disillusioned world.

Yet hope survives in the "little protected enclave" of childhood.[3] Defeated and disillusioned, Ludovic is still impatient to explain the complexities of the world to his young son Toto:

> Dépêche-toi. Je t'attends avec impatience, Toto . . . Tu n'en finis plus d'être petit. (NPG. 158)

Old soldiers never surrender and even in a time of resignation to defeated ideals, there is always hope that a new age will bring a new heroism and a new victory over the inevitable disillusionment of life.

[1] Vandromme, op. cit., p. 221.
[2] Ginestier, *Anouilh*, p. 110.
[3] Joan's description of her home village, Domrémy, where she first saw her visions. (PC. 13)

VII. La Grotte

"Généralement, c'est dans les pièces qu'on n'arrive pas à écrire qu'on avait le plus de choses à dire." (L'Auteur, *La Grotte*)

"Le dramaturge est prisonnier des contingences du théâtre et de la société: le caractère de son art est essentiellement social." (H. Ghéon, *L'Art du théâtre*)

La Grotte is unique among Anouilh's plays. It is a play which claims not to be a play at all, in the sense of a finished work of art, because its author has never been able to complete it:

Ce qu'on va jouer ce soir, c'est une pièce que je n'ai jamais pu écrire. (NPG. 165)

Accordingly, we are presented not with a play in the normal way but with a series of individual scenes and fragments, linked or separated by interventions, explanations and excuses from L'Auteur who is there on stage among the other characters.

As we might expect from an unwritten play it has no beginning. When the curtain rises all the characters are standing onstage, among them L'Auteur who steps forward and in a long monologue makes his excuses, introduces the characters, explains the unusual décor and sketches the situation of this play that he has been unable to finish, and which he intended to call *La Grotte*.

The action takes place in a private mansion in the exclusive Faubourg Saint-Germain at the turn of the century. It is a picture of life above and below stairs at that time, the grotto or cavern of the title being the kitchen and servants' quarters of the house. The unusual and striking décor reflects the play's content. It is made up of two levels. The stage level represents the kitchens and servants' quarters while above, on a raised wooden platform, is an elegant drawing-room. The two sets are linked by a wooden staircase. In the middle of the lower level is an immense kitchen stove from which a large black pipe passes up incongruously through the drawing-room. The action shifts from level to level with the help of a liberal use of blackouts and spot lighting.

Apart from this cumbersome set the only things clear in L'Auteur's mind are the various characters involved and the fact that the cook Marie-Jeanne has been murdered by a person or persons unknown; unknown, that is, even to L'Auteur. For want of a proper beginning, L'Auteur decides to present the original opening scene of the play, written before he abandoned the project in despair. This turns out to be a fairly unimaginative beginning in which the traditional police inspector, the Commissaire, arrives to start his investigation by interviewing the head of the household, Count Thibaut. The play continues in this fashion as other scenes are acted out on a try-and-see basis, interspersed by comments from L'Auteur. The circumstances surrounding Marie-Jeanne's death are gradually reconstructed. It transpires that, thirty years previously, Marie-Jeanne had an affair with her employer, the Count, and that her son, the Séminariste, was the product of this affair. When the Séminariste returns home to his new job he falls in love with the kitchen-maid, Adèle. Adèle, however, is already pregnant, having been raped by the coachman Léon, and Marie-Jeanne is helping her to induce a miscarriage. Adèle is afraid to divulge the name of her attacker since Léon is Marie-Jeanne's present lover. Adèle is also being badgered by the valet Marcel, evidently a pimp in his spare time, who is trying to pressurize her to take a job in an Algerian brothel. Adèle is one of life's downtrodden unfortunates who, even at her age, can already look back on a life of degradation in service. The Séminariste begs the Countess to do something to honour Adèle and, together, they decide to ask her to be godmother to the Countess's new-born son. This event is arranged with due ceremony. All the servants are lined up below stairs while the Countess descends in procession to present her new baby to Adèle. As the moment approaches the unwilling Adèle becomes hysterical and screams obscenities at the Countess, letting slip in the process the name of her attacker, Léon. Pandemonium ensues. When calm returns Marie-Jeanne turns to confront Léon. Both draw knives and the Séminariste steps in to separate them. There is a sudden blackout and when the lights come on again Marie-Janne has been stabbed. She is laid out on the kitchen table and dies soon afterwards of her wounds. At the last moment the Commissaire appears and announces to L'Auteur that he has the culprit—Léon:

> Au fond, vous voyez, elle était toute simple, votre histoire. C'est vous qui aviez tendance à la compliquer. (NPG. 292)

Some critics have been unfair to *La Grotte* in seeing it as little more than "a clever mystery play"[1] or "a whimsical effort . . . a picture already familiar from Anouilh's earlier plays, where it is

[1] Archer, op. cit., p. 42.

handled with greater strength and a less self-conscious theatricality".[1] But *La Grotte* is not as "capricious"[2] a work as it might seem. Obviously the presentation of the play as unwritten is a literary device to help Anouilh make the points he wishes to and the same thought and planning have gone into it as into all Anouilh's plays. It presents more of a puzzle, perhaps, on a first encounter than other plays but, as L'Auteur reminds us at the outset:

Le théâtre, c'est une partie où le public reçoit, une fois sur deux, le ballon sur la tête; si le ballon tombe dans un coin de la salle où il y a des maladroits qui ne savent pas le renvoyer, la partie n'est pas bonne, voilà tout. Mais nous, nous nous sommes entraînés, six semaines, pas vous. (NPG. 166)

This is a familiar challenge or appeal to us from Anouilh, and, in the case of *La Grotte*, it is particularly worth accepting. The play is rich in meaning but not obscure. After all, for the first time in Anouilh's work we have an author onstage to explain his problems to us and guide us, as best he can, through the play. We cannot explore all the implications of the issues it raises because the aesthetic matters it deals with are set against the wide background of changes in society and thought which have taken place in the twentieth century. Those matters we can pursue, within present limits, have a double interest. *La Grotte*, like *L'Invitation au château*, is a play in which Anouilh pauses to take stock and reappraise his own work. It will then help us understand Anouilh's own view of his intentions and achievements. At the same time it is a play about writing a play by one of the most gifted and prolific of modern French dramatists, and its lessons are also of more general interest and significance.

The first of these concerns the dramatist's relationship to his inspiration. In this, *La Grotte* reminds us of *L'Invitation au château* where Anouilh dramatized, in Horace and Frédéric, different tendencies within his own inspiration. This is also the first of the dramatist's many difficulties here in *La Grotte*. L'Auteur would have preferred, in ideal circumstances, to write only "une histoire très simple et très pure" (NPG. 184). He is repeatedly appalled at the bad taste into which several of his scenes degenerate, and after the fiasco of the Countess's descent into the kitchen he loses his nerve:

Je ne peux pas croire que la vie soit aussi laide que cela. Il y a tout de

[1] Pronko, op. cit., preface to the second edition, p. (xiv).
[2] Borgal, op. cit., p. 169.

même des braves gens partout. C'est un devoir de le dire et d'écrire des pièces où il y a des braves gens et des bons sentiments. *Il hurle comme un fou:* Il faut travailler dans les bons sentiments, rien que dans les bons sentiments! Et tant pis pour la littérature! Il n'y a que les hommes de lettres qui se figurent qu'elle a de l'importance. (NPG. 279)

This is reminiscent of Anouilh's own, often stated view of himself as an entertainer, providing work for actors who, in turn, help audiences to escape for a time from the worries and anxieties of everyday life.[1] But there is a difficulty in this which Anouilh experienced with *La Valse des Toréadors*, in which he invited us to "rire avec lui . . . de tout ce qu'il pouvait constater de désolant et d'absurde dans la condition humaine".[2] Many did not laugh at *La Valse des Toréadors*, which they found to be in extreme bad taste. Despite L'Auteur's hope that life cannot be all that ugly, *La Grotte* is, if anything, in even worse taste than *La Valse des Toréadors*. As critics have noted, the play seems to go out of its way to emphasize the uglier side of life.[3] It is a panorama of human cruelty and iniquity, involving poverty and hardship, white slavery and prostitution, rape and murder.

The obvious solution for L'Auteur, then, would be to have the courage of his own convictions and ignore this seamier side of life. But things are not that simple. L'Auteur's convictions about the theatre's function and his inspiration are clearly in conflict. He may dismiss the importance of literature but he has not renounced the search for truth. The central character of *La Grotte* as he explains is Marie-Jeanne and it is to bring her to life that he conceived *La Grotte* in the first place.[4] And Marie-Jeanne is not an ingredient of some inoffensive bedtime story. In his personal notes L'Auteur calls her "Notre Mère la terre" (NPG. 183) and in his mind she is "un personnage énorme, un Falstaff femelle. Quelque chose de shakespearien" (NPG. 221). L'Auteur intends her to be an image of humanity of all its courage, tenacity and resourcefulness in adversity and its "ancient pride" in subservience. "Queen of the Grotto" and "old mother nature", she is a symbol with mythological overtones.[5] Clearly then L'Auteur's ambitions in *La Grotte* go far beyond a simple story. He is trying to create an image of mankind in its many

[1] *Opéra*, March 7th 1951; *L'Avant-Scène*, Dec. 15th 1959; *International Herald* Tribune, Sept. 18th 1970; *Le Figaro*, Nov. 29th 1972.

[2] *Le Figaro*, Jan. 23rd 1952.

[3] Harvey, op. cit., p. 146; Borgal, op. cit., p. 167.

[4] NPG. 183.

[5] NPG. 183, 185, 258.

contradictory facets, and that means harsh as well as tender, ugly as well as admirable.

The deepest wells of his inspiration, then, pull him in directions away from his convictions about what the theatre should be doing. We see this at those moments when he is genuinely sorry for the hurt he is inflicting on his characters:

> Ah Adèle! C'est ma tristesse et mon remords. Tout ce qui va lui arriver, je le porte sur mon dos comme une honte. Je n'aurais peut-être pas dû lui faire comprendre certaines choses; cela aurait été plus simple pour elle. (NPG. 196)

The same point is made when the Séminariste approaches L'Auteur as spokesman for the other characters and asks to be allowed to continue their story without further interruption:

> Il ne fallait m'inventer et m'inventer ce destin et cette mère et faire naître ma honte . . . Pour vous, ce n'était qu'un caprice de votre imagination, vous étiez en train de faire votre métier, vous cherchiez à construire une pièce. Vous n'auriez peut-être pas dû, mais vous l'avez fait. Alors maintenant, il faut nous laisser. Ne plus intervenir jusqu'à la fin. (NPG. 261)

Why indeed, a clerical student in the first place? L'Auteur asks himself the same question:

> Il y a déjà assez d'histoires épineuses dans cette sacrée pièce. Eh bien! non! C'est un séminariste. Il va falloir que vous le subissiez comme je l'ai subi. (NPG. 169)

This helplessness of the creator before his own creation expressed in his characters' independence is, like the unwritten nature of *La Grotte*, a literary pose. But it also expresses a profound psychological truth which has been experienced and noted by other writers. The idea will be familiar to readers of Pirandello and Anouilh is not original in stating it. It remains nonetheless at the origins of a lot of L'Auteur's difficulties in *La Grotte*.

Anouilh's interest in character should be clear by now. He has often underlined the importance of character as a focus of dramatic interest and stressed that an ability to create character is the mark of a true dramatist.[1] He has practised what he preaches over the years by forsaking realistic plots and careful construction, placing his faith in character creation, and building his plays around character interest. The character is not so much in the play as the play is in the character. This is precisely the source of L'Auteur's diffi-

[1] Vandromme, op. cit., p. 187; *Opéra*, loc. cit., *Arts*, May 1st 1957; *Les Nouvelles Littéraires*, Feb 5th 1959.

culties with character in *La Grotte*. He shares Anouilh's belief in the importance of character but each character is a potential play in itself:

Tous les personnages étaient importants dans cette histoire. C'est à cause de cela que je n'arrivais pas à l'écrire. Il aurait fallu un sujet de pièce, avec tous ses développements, pour chacun d'eux. (NPG. 196)

L'Auteur's interest is clearly in character above all else. Of Marie-Jeanne he admits:

C'est pour essayer de la faire revivre, pour la faire sortir du monde vague des idées possibles et lui donner, avec mon faible pouvoir, deux sous de réalité, que j'avais voulu écrire cette pièce. (NPG. 183)

When he confesses a similar ambition for Adèle his problems are clear.[1] On the one hand, there are the needs and demands of his characters, each with its own role:

Vous avez tous des rôles, vous le savez bien. (NPG. 185)

On the other hand, there is the need for some degree of internal order and organization within the play, and the subordination of parts within a coherent whole. This need is implicit in all L'Auteur's problems and a basic assumption of *La Grotte*. But we may well wonder if L'Auteur is creating problems where there are none. The logical conclusion of his interest in character would be to ignore all other constraints and write a play containing nothing but characters. L'Auteur has, however, already thought of this:

J'aurais souhaité qu'il n'y eût pas de décor, rien que des personnages dans cette pièce. Mais, cela s'est révélé impossible. (NPG. 168)

The décor represents a situation—an elegant household at a given time in history—and this in turn suggests a relationship between the characters, that of servant to master. In other words, L'Auteur is saying that he found it impossible to create characters and make them express themselves without placing them in some kind of situation. There is perhaps no absolute reason why this should be so but it is extremely difficult, if not impossible, to conceive of the notion of character in a vacuum. Characters exist only through what they say and do and a character is the sum of its attitudes and actions, past, present and future. It is through those attitudes and actions that we understand the character. In other words, there is always some kind of situation or story, no matter how rudimentary, implicit in the existence of a character. Moreover, the theatre is a

[1] NPG. 196.

particularly social and communal art form, in which we participate to discover images of ourselves and truths about our existence. We understand its characters, as we understand ourselves and others, in relation to the situation in which they find themselves.

Count Thibaut in *La Grotte*, for example, is a figure who believes in the status quo and never steps out of his own social position and role to transgress class barriers. Like Anouilh's earlier aristocrats, Tigre and Ornifle, he also maintains a deliberately facile, playful approach to life and abhors earnestness and seriousness. But the Count's present character is determined by his past experience when he did go below stairs and fall in love with his cook Marie-Jeanne. The resulting hurt and unhappiness for all involved has convinced him that to upset social structures or become emotionally involved with life can only have disastrous consequences. In the light of his own experience he advises his wife strongly against making the same mistake. The outcome of her well-intentioned action only seems to justify his views. Where you have characters, then, you have stories and if L'Auteur is to develop his characters and allow them to express themselves he must tell their stories. But he cannot tell all their stories within the practical limits imposed by the play and the theatre, whence the conflict between character and construction.

The ubiquitous Commissaire, who is always at L'Auteur's elbow, reminding him of his obligations towards the audience and warning him of their impatience and impending boredom, represents an extreme solution to L'Auteur's dilemma. He is the representative of a literary genre, the detective story, in which the emphasis is on action and tight, logical construction of the plot. Appropriately, he advocates a strong story-line and the maintenance of dramatic interest by mystery and suspense.[1] This solution is clearly unacceptable to L'Auteur because it would subordinate character entirely to the development of the plot. It would also limit the significance of the play. Truth for the Commissaire is confined to discovering who killed the cook. Needless to say, L'Auteur is interested in a higher order of truth than that.

L'Auteur dismisses the Commissaire as "un personnage artificiel, une raclure du vieux boulevard" (NPG. 240), but the Commissaire has a significance in *La Grotte* which belies his appearance. In one sense the detective element in *La Grotte* is a completely false trail. The real subject of the play is not who killed Marie-Jeanne but the picture of social conditions and human relationships which surround the murder and contribute to it. We are not even sure who killed

[1] NPG. 197.

Marie-Jeanne since the stage is blacked out at the all-important moment. The Commissaire comes up with a culprit, the brutal coachman Léon, but this is the kind of conventional suspect we find in the least imaginative type of detective story. Furthermore his confession was extracted by what the Commissaire euphemistically calls "the American method" (NPG. 292) so we may be doubly sceptical about its value. The fact we do not know for sure the exact circumstances of Marie-Jeanne's stabbing does not prevent our enjoyment of the play nor our appreciation of its meaning. The very fact that this is so, however, puts the Commissaire in a more authoritative position than we might suspect. In describing the audience as "un petit curieux" (NPG. 197) he is expressing a profound truth in his own language. There is a coherent meaning behind the play despite its unfinished appearance:

> Je sais très bien ce que j'ai voulu dire avec cette Grotte. Ce n'est pas parce que je n'ai pas pu arriver à écrire la pièce que je ne le sais pas. (NPG. 240)

We can reconstruct that meaning by piecing together the various episodes and fragments which remain on this unwritten story. Ironically we are in fact doing exactly what the Commissaire is trying to do—piece together the bits of information available to get at the meaning of the whole thing! So while L'Auteur dismisses the Commissaire as the kind of artificial character "qui n'a rien à voir avec l'histoire; et que je mets toujours dans mes pièces pour m'aider à commencer" (NPG. 169) the Commissaire represents a more important part of the dramatic process, from the audience's point of view, than L'Auteur seems to realize. Finally, Anouilh takes a more circumspect, not to say ambiguous, stance on the whole issue of plot construction and suspense. L'Auteur dismisses loftily the Commissaire's recommendations in this respect, but *La Grotte* is, after all, constructed like a murder mystery. We are told at the beginning that Marie-Jeanne has been murdered but Anouilh is careful to keep the murder scene until near the end of the play. What's more, by denying us the identity of the killer at the last moment and making us realize he has been leading us along a false trail he plays the kind of clever trick typical of the best mystery writers.

La Grotte is not a dissertation but a working demonstration of some of the problems and difficulties encountered by a working dramatist. We have concentrated on two of these, both key aspects, central to Anouilh's own practice. The conflicts in L'Auteur's inspiration and intentions underline the obstacles to his own view of the theatre as a game or *divertissement* and L'Auteur's organizational difficulties are a reduction to fundamentals of Anouilh's own activities in exploiting character at the expense of plot. *La Grotte* is only one more example of that continuous aesthetic debate and unrelenting self-criticism which is apparent throughout Anouilh's work. It differs from other plays only in that it deals more overtly with these matters. But the issues raised in *La Grotte* have wider implications. Anouilh's return to fundamentals in *La Grotte*, coming when it does, suggests he is looking again at his own art in the light of developments in French theatre in the fifties. This decade saw the rise of the post-war avant-garde theatre and the appearance on the theatrical scene of Beckett and Ionesco.

Anouilh has a better record in relation to avant-garde theatre than some of those who dismiss him as outdated in comparison to it. When *Waiting for Godot* was first produced in Paris in 1953 Anouilh recognized Beckett's genius and saw in the play as great a milestone in the modern theatre as Pitoëff's production of Pirandello's *Six Characters in search of an Author* in 1923.[1] In 1956, while his own *Ornifle* was playing at the Comédie des Champs-Élysées, Anouilh urged theatre-goers not to miss the play next door at the Studio des Champs-Élysées. It was Ionesco's *Les Chaises*.[2]

A parody of avant-garde theatre appears for the first time in Anouilh in *L'Hurluberlu*, in the form of a play by the new young author Popopief: *Zim! Boum! ou Julien l'Apostat. Antidrame*. This reveals Anouilh's devastating gifts for parody but it is light-hearted. Behind *La Grotte* lies a more thoughtful appraisal of the issues raised by the new Avant-garde. The *L'Hurluberlu* parody singles out two of these. The first is the new theatre's rejection of 'play':

> Le théâtre moderne a fait un grand pas en avant. Le jeu pur, le divertissement, c'est fini! (NPG. 87)

We have already seen that the General is far from convinced by David Edward's enthusiasm for the new tragedy and *L'Hurluberlu* reaffirms Anouilh's view of the theatre as game. Even so, he recognizes in *La Grotte* that the game can never be entirely innocent or divorced from reality, for two reasons. The ingredients or raw materials of the game are life, with all its unpleasantness, and the dramatist himself cannot renounce the highest ambitions of his art to reveal the truth about themselves and their existence to his fellow men.

Anouilh is closer in spirit to the new avant-garde theatre in its

[1] *Arts*, Feb. 27th 1953.
[2] Vandromme, op. cit., p. 233.

reactions against excessive plotting and story-telling and over-careful construction. He classes himself proudly among the broader modern movement who, in the footsteps of Pirandello, have been trying to "étrangler l'anecdote" and kill the well-made play.[1] But again he takes a circumspect, if not pessimistic, view in *La Grotte*.

We can never fully reduce the anecdotal side of the theatre because it is inherent in the nature of character and necessary to its development. Indeed, one of the lessons of *La Grotte* is that no matter how much the dramatist may do to distort plot and destroy careful construction, his audience will always reconstruct the edifice and impose their own order in the search for meaning. On the wider issue of innovation in general Anouilh is ambiguous. He puts Beckett and Ionesco among the great innovators of the twentieth century while arguing that both really have their roots in an older and more constant theatrical tradition than the Avant-garde.[2] Moreover, he is keenly aware that all innovations quickly become clichés and conventions in their turn. He has gone as far as possible from the well-made play in presenting an unmade play, but the final irony of *La Grotte* is indicated from the outset:

J'entends un critique qui dit à l'oreille de son voisin qu'il a déjà vu cela dans Pirandello. (NPG. 166, 167)

It may not be exactly the same thing, as L'Auteur claims, but the unmade play has become as much a characteristic form of twentieth-century theatre as the well-made play was of the nineteenth century. Still, art, like life, goes on. Artists in each generation come up against the same perennial problems as their predecessors and they achieve the same partial and relative successes. Nonetheless, as Anouilh remarks on L'Auteur's final exit at the end of *La Grotte*:

Il faut espérer qu'on l'applaudit quand même. (NPG. 292)

[1] *Opéra*, loc. cit.
[2] *Arts*, loc. cit.; Vandromme, op. cit., p. 232; *International Herald Tribune*, loc. cit.

VIII. The Play as Pretext

Ne réveillez pas Madame – Le Boulanger – Cher Antoine – Les Poissons rouges – Tu étais si gentil – Le Directeur de l'Opéra – L'Arrestation – Le Scénario – Chers Zoiseaux – La Culotte

"Nous sommes tous les metteurs en scène omnipotents et inopérants, la plupart du temps, d'un opéra intime: notre vie." (Anouilh)

After the production of *La Grotte* in 1961 the usually prolific Anouilh fell silent. The Parisian public, for whom a new Anouilh play was almost an annual occurrence, did not see another until the production of *Le Boulanger, la boulangère et le petit mitron* in 1968.[1] In retrospect, this silence is not surprising, coming in the wake of *La Grotte*. It marks Anouilh's second major reappraisal of his work and the beginning of a new, third phase in his evolution.

His silence can be attributed, in his own words, to "mille raisons, à la fois privées et publiques".[2] Chief among public reasons was the return to power in 1958 of De Gaulle, to whom Anouilh had "une opposition sentimentale profonde",[3] dating from the events of the Liberation:

> J'ai été joué pendant qu'il était au pouvoir. J'ai arrêté d'écrire et je ne voulais pas être joué dans des théâtres officiels comme la Comédie-Française. Cela, je ne le voulais pas.[4]

It was De Gaulle who refused a plea for mercy on Robert Brasillach's behalf and confirmed the death sentence. Anouilh's protest was not just at the death of Brasillach, however, but at the general injustice and inhumanity of the *épuration* with which he evidently associated De Gaulle.

Among personal reasons, the educational needs of a growing family meant that Anouilh could spend less time during the summer in his Swiss chalet-retreat where the major part of his creative writing is done.[5] This interruption of his routine was nothing if not

[1] *L'Orchestre* and *La Foire d'empoigne* were produced in 1962 but date from 1957 and 1958 respectively. *Becket* was revived in 1966.
[2] *Paris-Match*, Oct. 21st 1972.
[3] ibid.
[4] ibid.
[5] *Le Figaro*, Dec. 31st 1963.

timely. By the beginning of the sixties Anouilh was growing weary of the vicissitudes and uncertainties of a long theatrical career, and particularly of his treatment by the Parisian critics:

Se faire éreinter comme je l'ai été, ça fait mal, croyez-moi.[1]

He retaliated by voicing his disgust at the reception of his own plays and his dissatisfaction with the general critical climate prevailing in the capital. Using one of his favourite metaphors for the theatre, he declared:

Vous invitez des gens à dîner, ils crachent dans vos plats. Un beau jour, vous vous dites que ce n'est plus la peine de leur faire la cuisine. C'est ce que je me suis dit.[2]

However justified he was in attacking his critics, Anouilh also felt himself that the time was right to reappraise his own work:

Moi, j'ai bien créé un choc mais un choc répété 25 fois, il est usé. Une coupure s'est produite, accentuée. Je ne voulais plus écrire . . .[3]

Even so, his retirement was more a gesture than a reality. The early sixties are marked by a flurry of activity on Anouilh's part as adaptor and producer of other people's work.[4] Moreover, his real silence lasted only two or three years. In 1964, he was already writing *Ne réveillez pas Madame* and in 1968, when *Le Boulanger* reached the stage, Anouilh admitted it was already three years old and that he had a backlog of plays awaiting production.[5]

The reality behind Anouilh's silence in no way detracts from its significance as a time of self-scrutiny. In his own opinion, *Le Boulanger* is a marked change of direction in his work and these new plays are "tout à fait différentes."[6] We must treat such statements circumspectly, of course. This period is distinguished by its own characteristic themes and a new dramatic form. But these are also the extension or amplification of features and interests which are already familiar from earlier years.

The most striking development of this period is the presence onstage of a professional man of letters in the main role. This carries on the example of *La Grotte*, but there has, in fact, almost always been some kind of organizer or master of ceremonies in Anouilh's plays from the beginning. In his earlier plays this was most often an

[1] *Le Monde*, Nov. 1st 1966.
[2] ibid.
[3] *L'Aurore*, May 2nd 1968.
[4] See Appendix for chronology of Anouilh's professional life in the sixties.
[5] *Les Nouvelles Littéraires*, Nov. 14th 1958.
[6] *L'Express*, Oct. 9th 1967.

eccentric old duchess. In the middle period it was the amateur producer Tigre. A professional writer appears for the first time in *Ornifle*. In seven out of the ten plays Anouilh has written since *La Grotte* an individual with a professional connection of some kind to literature or the theatre appears. Chief representative of this new man is the aristocrat and playwright Antoine de Saint-Flour who appears in *Cher Antoine* and *Les Poissons rouges*. He changes nationality in *Le Directeur de l'Opéra* and becomes Antonio di San Floura, a director of an Italian opera house. Julien in *Ne réveillez pas Madame* is also a man of the theatre, an actor-manager with his own theatre and troupe. We forsake the theatre for the cinema in *Le Scénario* where two scriptwriters, a young idealist and an older, disillusioned man, also of aristocratic origins, are struggling to complete a scenario on the eve of the Second World War. The hero in *Chers Zoiseaux* is a writer of cheap, trashy, but very successful detective stories and, in Anouilh's most recent play, *La Culotte*, his hero Léon has been elevated to the French Academy.

This literary figure is also a family man and the trials and tensions of family life form the most dominant and central theme of the period. While not suggesting any strict autobiographical parallel, Anouilh's heroes and their circumstances have noticeably evolved along with his own. His heroes are now mostly middle-aged, successful writers, surrounded by grown-up families and even grandchildren in Le Chef's case, in *Chers Zoiseaux*. At the same time, the influence of the family is one of Anouilh's oldest and most enduring themes. Only the perspective has changed. Marc in *Jézabel* and Thérèse in *La Sauvage* were the children of unhappy families. Now we are seeing things from the viewpoint of a besieged father. Questioned about this renewed emphasis on the family, Anouilh replied:

> Tout le monde vit de la famille, des enfants et des femmes . . . Les enfants, j'en ai eu beaucoup et c'est très difficile à élever. On rate ses enfants comme on rate ses amours. Il faut avoir du talent pour être amoureux, pour être père.[1]

Those could be the sentiments of almost any of Anouilh's heroes in this period. Family life is as chaotic as it ever was for the Generals in Chapter Five and, despite his growing number of dependants, the hero remains a lonely figure. Young Toto, the General's son in *Ardèle* and *L'Hurluberlu*, has grown up in *Le Directeur de l'Opéra* and *La Culotte* into an angry, spoilt and selfish young man whose relationship with his father consists of taking money and offering

[1] *Paris-Match*, loc. cit.

insults in return. The family, in its creator's eyes, is a kind of voracious monster, eating up his time, attention, tranquillity and money. The hero finds himself the object of constant recrimination, by his wife for his neglect, indifference, selfishness and philandering, and by his children who, well acquainted with Freudian theory, blame their selfish, rebellious behaviour on an unhappy upbringing.

The hero in *Chers Zoiseaux* has given up writing out of disgust at the ease with which he can churn out his cheap paperback thrillers. But he is obliged to take up his pen once more to support his disorderly and parasitical household, the "chers zoiseaux" of the title. These include a Marxist son-in-law, a daughter always en route to a demonstration or protest march and two sexually precocious and insubordinate granddaughters. As if all this were not enough, the house is besieged by an anarchist bookseller, with bombs and machine-guns, whose daughter has been taken advantage of by Le Chef's son-in-law. Le Chef's problems are solved with a bang when a bomb which his granddaughters are tossing about explodes.

Antonio in *Le Directeur de l'Opéra* has found a less dramatic answer to his problems. He has moved out and taken up residence in his office at the Opera House where he is looked after by his bookkeeper, Impossibile. Even there, however, he is not safe from the demands of a car-crashing son, a daughter who makes a habit of committing suicide and a wife with an unending need for housekeeping money. When a strike is declared in his home-from-home he proves to be just as effectual in controlling disorder there as at home.

In *La Culotte* this process of recrimination against the hero is carried to its ultimate conclusion. The play is set in the France of the very near future where there has been another French Revolution and the Women's Liberation Movement is in power. Under the new laws Léon is arraigned before the Committee of Liberated Women for his misdeeds. He is acquitted of making the maid pregnant when her baby turns out to be black but there still remains other charges to answer, the same eternal complaints from an unhappy wife and children that his other counterparts have to endure. He is duly condemned for his crimes but manages to escape punishment at the last moment by taking refuge in Switzerland, where the Revolution has not reached—yet. It would be wrong to think, however, that the hero is an entirely innocent victim. Antonio asks himself:

Cette famille dévorante, dont je me plains, que lui aurais-je donné, moi, au juste, quand on fera les comptes? (PBQ. 313)

At the heart of all these unhappy families lies an unhappy marriage. Husband and wife indulge in bitter recriminations over mutual infidelity or indifference but they are basically protesting at the fragility of love in an imperfect world. In *Le Boulanger* Adolphe's young son asks him why he and mummy are always quarrelling. Is it because they do not love each other? No, replies his father, it is because we have loved each other.[1] Most to blame for the failure of these relationships is the isolation and egoism of the individual.

Moi! Moi! J'existe moi! (PBQ. 55)

is the battle-cry of the wives in particular, but both partners are to blame, and both are equally selfish in their own ways. If the wives are self-preoccupied and unfaithful it is to some extent the result of their husbands' neglect. Among the faults for which the dramatist-hero reproaches himself in these plays is his absorption in his *métier* at the expense of his wife and family. When Aglaé reminds Julien that he has taken her dancing twice in ten years, Julien admits:

J'avais ce théâtre . . . Toute ma vie s'est passée entre ces portants. Mes bals c'était ceux de mes pièces. (PBQ. 159)

Anouilh is not just rehashing familiar themes in this period. He is, after a long experience of both the theatre and life, reaffirming the importance of the family as the prime, basic and universal influence upon the individual. If there were fewer unhappy families there would be fewer unhappy, maladjusted individuals. Anouilh has often been accused of complacency and indulgence for his bourgeois audience but, in this respect, he pulls no punches. His preface to *Le Boulanger* is a hard-hitting indictment of the bourgeois family in respect of parental neglect and the child's unhappiness. That conviction is also clearly illustrated by the play itself. Adolphe and Élodie are a middle-aged couple who escape continually into daydreams to compensate for the boredom, disillusion and dissatisfaction of their marriage. When they do share a moment of reality together it is inevitably to bicker and quarrel. Caught between them is their young son Toto, who has in turn learned the trick of escaping into his own childish make-believe from the unhappy atmosphere at home. As he reads his school history book he dreams of belonging to a happy family group like that of Louis XVI, Marie-Antoinette and their son when in prison together during the Revolution. The people nicknamed them the baker, the baker's wife and the little

[1] NPG. 371.

baker's boy when they escorted them back from Versailles to a hunger-ridden Paris—whence the title of Anouilh's play.

Anouilh sees this childhood unhappiness in a long and depressing perspective. Julien in *Ne réveillez pas Madame* is actor-director of his own troupe, which also includes his present wife Aglaé and her lover Bachman. From the sentimental plays about ideal family life he chooses and the parts in which he casts himself, his wife and her lover, it is clear that he is trying to relive life on the stage as it never was in reality. Son of a promiscuous actress mother, his life has been marred by an unhappy neglected childhood. This in turn has left him an unhappy and maladjusted adult, unable to form stable, lasting relationships in his own right. As the play shifts from present to past and back again, we realize that Julien has been trying, through his two successive marriages, to win in his wives the love denied him by his mother when he was a child. Julien is condemned to fight over and over again that fight for affection begun in childhood. We see this in a striking scene which occurs during one of the flashbacks to Julien's childhood. He is the cause of a quarrel between his mother and her lover Alberto which ends with his mother being beaten. Julien the child throws himself at Alberto in his mother's defence and Julien the adult who has been watching this flashback from the wings, rushes to the aid of his young self:

> La lumière change; en se battant, l'acteur (Alberto) a perdu ses moustaches, son col trop haut: c'est Bachman maintenant avec qui Julien se bat quand tout le monde entre en courant pour les séparer. (PBQ. 221)

The frustrations of childhood remain with us and prevent or delay full maturity. Ironically, the unhappy child in Julien, which is still looking for the kind of ideal mother-son relationship he has never known, sabotages his relationships with two wives. So Julien creates the same conditions within his own family as he himself experienced as a child. Childhood unhappiness is handed down from generation to generation. Unhappy children make unhappy parents who make more unhappy children.

This view of human development has led Anouilh to reflect on time, which is the second major preoccupation of this period. Again, this is not an entirely new aspect of Anouilh's drama. There has always been a temporal dimension to his heroes' and heroines' rejection of life. What they were rebelling against was the passage of time and the inevitable disillusioning effect that growing old would have on their ideals. In these plays people grow old but they do not grow up. Time is an illusion which masks the fact that, despite the outward appearance of change, we progress little if at all, in our inner lives, from the unhappy, frustrated children that we were. Our distinction between past and present is "un trompe-l'œil qui nous abuse, sur le moment" (NPG. 547) because "on attache toujours une importance exagérée au présent" (PS. 156). We view our lives, forwards and backwards, from the present moment but we need only step out of the flux of time to see that this is a false perspective. Tonton, the old prompter in *Ne réveillez pas Madame*, has stepped aside from the flow of time. For him time has stopped. As he shuffles back and forth to his prompter's box, he reminisces continually about his heydays before the First World War when, in his prime, he danced the cake-walk and made endless easy conquests. He realizes that:

comme on s'obstine à barboter dans le courant au lieu de regarder couler l'eau du fleuve, on est victime d'illusions d'optique. (PBQ. 174)

The deliberately non-chronological and fragmented presentation of the action in many of these plays and the frequent use of flash-backs keep us standing on the bank of the river of time. As we do so we realize that:

C'est tout en même temps. Et c'est toujours la même chose. (PBQ. 222)

Les Poissons rouges takes place on Bastille Day, the fourteenth of July, 1960 and in the author's head. It chronicles a day in the life of Antoine de Saint-Flour, playwright, who has not had the same success in his private life over the years as he has had in the theatre. He now spends his time defending himself against the reproaches of an unhappy wife, an envious and embittered friend, a suicide-prone mistress and a pregnant fifteen-year-old daughter who views her forthcoming marriage as an escape from an unhappy home. Reproach seems to have been the story of Antoine's life ever since that distant day when his grandmother caught him urinating in the goldfish bowl. Like *Le Boulanger*, the play becomes a mixture of reality, fantasy and flashback as Antoine remembers scenes, characters and incidents from the past and even imagines his own execution during the *épuration* in 1944. In one particular sequence, half-dream, half-nightmare, his whole married life from newly-wed bliss to his daughter's unhappy marriage is accelerated and compressed into one night.[1]

The irrelevance of time in our inner, emotional lives is illustrated in even more remarkable fashion by the structure of *L'Arrestation*. It is an enigmatic play at first sight, a kind of jigsaw puzzle in time

[1] NPG. 555–565.

which we are left to assemble into a meaningful picture as best we can. To add to the mystery, the characters are designated simply as L'Homme, Le Jeune Homme, Le Petit, La Mère, La Jeune Femme and so forth. All is revealed in the end, however, and we realize with hindsight that the play is strewn with generous hints throughout. L'Homme, Le Jeune Homme and Le Petit, who often share the stage simultaneously, are all one and the same person at different times in his life. He is a notorious criminal on the run whose car has crashed during a police chase. What we are watching on stage is the thoughts and memories of his past life as they flash through his mind during the last moments of consciousness. Most of the action takes place out of season in the run-down Casino of a once elegant resort where the hero spent many summers as a child. In this setting he relives the happy and unhappy moments of his childhood, his unhappy marriage and the affair with a young slut which started him off on a life of crime.

The time theme and the sense of life's essential immutability which lies behind it brings Anouilh to refine his ideas on the relationship of theatre to life. The theatrical nature of real life is the basic working premise of all Anouilh's drama and he has portrayed life variously as heroic, tragic, farcical and grotesque. In these years Anouilh introduces an all-important distinction between the outer and the inner theatricality of life. For Anouilh life is, and remains, thoroughly theatrical; but the obvious visible theatricality of life is not its true theatricality. Antoine explains in *Cher Antoine*:

> Cela a l'air d'être le Châtelet,[1] la vie, parce qu'il y a toujours beaucoup de bruit et de figurants, mais à la fin, on s'aperçoit qu'il n'y avait que quatre ou cinq acteurs et que la pièce était secrète, derrière tant de coups de théâtre inutiles. (PBQ. 47)

What Antoine calls the hidden play or *pièce secrète* of life, is that basic drama into which we are all born and which affects us throughout our lives—the family situation. The four or five characters of which it consists are the father and mother, son and/or daughter, lover and/or mistress. What part we play depends on our age, sex and circumstances. We see in *Ne réveillez pas Madame* that unhappy sons grow up to be unhappy husbands and fathers and other women's lovers in an unending search for true love and affection. Likewise, unhappy daughters become dissatisfied wives and neglectful mothers, and other men's mistresses. We may not play all these parts, but the basic influences of the family situation form us for

[1] A Parisian variety theatre known for its spectacular productions.

life. The secret or hidden nature of this central drama presents a problem for the dramatist who is trying to capture onstage "cet instant de théâtre . . . où la vérité de l'homme va surgir".[1] He has no difficulty reproducing the theatrical appearance of real life, but how does he convey the true inner theatrical essence of life when it is not at all theatrical in appearance and when "le vrai texte (est) celui qu'on ne dit jamais" (PBQ. 111)?

Cher Antoine illustrates the hiatus between the outer theatrical appearance of life and its true theatrical essence, and demonstrates the dramatist's difficulties in trying to isolate and capture this essence. The Antoine of the title has in fact died before the play begins, although he does appear thanks to the same use of flashbacks as in the other plays of this period. His death is the reason for the play because the various people in his life—wives, children, mistresses, colleagues and friends—have been summoned by his lawyer to his last home, an old house high in the Bavarian Alps, to attend a memorial service and be present at the reading of his will. By a device Anouilh has used before the exposition is done deliberately in an obvious, straightforward manner. The guests are brought to the house in relays and, in between arrivals, discuss Antoine naturally enough and thus fill in the background for us. Anouilh is quite deliberately underlining the mechanics of the theatre. It is moreover meant to resemble a particular type of theatre. Not long after they arrive the 'unexpected' happens, in the form of an avalanche which effectively maroons the cast for the duration of the play. This is the kind of tried-and-tested device typical of late-nineteenth-century Boulevard theatre, the kind of high point which provided a suitable end to the first act in the well-made plays of Scribe and Sardou. In case this should be lost on us, Anouilh underlines it in an exchange between the theatre critic Cravatar and the veteran actress Carlotta:

CRAVATAR: Hé bien, cette fois, ça y est, nous sommes coincés! Antoine l'aura réussie encore une fois, sa fin d'acte! C'est l'avalanche! (*Il hurle au bord de l'hystérie*) C'est d'un mauvais goût! Ah, l'affreux théâtre!
CARLOTTA: C'est admirable! C'est du Sardou! (PBQ. 40)

It is extremely significant that the real substance of *Cher Antoine* should only begin to emerge in the time between this mock *fin d'acte*, typical of traditional Boulevard theatre, and the real end of the first act. Anouilh uses the whole last act of *Cher Antoine* to illustrate this same discrepancy between what we think of as a play and the real drama which lies beneath the surface of life. He has

[1] Anouilh's phrase in *Le Figaro*, Sept 29th 1966.

deliberately and courageously written a last act which gives the impression of having no interest or purpose other than tying up the loose ends and dispersing the cast in as conventional a way as they had been assembled. The real drama of Antoine's life has finished towards the end of Act III when he realizes the futility of his efforts to get at the truth of life:

on ne saura rien! On ne sait jamais rien. On meurt sans savoir. (PBQ. 117)

We learn that shortly after this failure, Antoine shot himself while cleaning his gun. It would appear to have been accidental.

There is, on the face of it, no need for such a failure and such pessimism. The dramatist need only, after all, adapt his style, making it less patently theatrical and more in keeping with the *pièce secrète* of life which he is trying to convey. But Antoine has thought of this and tried it unsuccessfully. Not long before his death he summons a group of actors from Paris to this unlikely location in Bavaria to rehearse a new play, which will be his last attempt to reveal the *pièce secrète* beneath the theatrical appearances of life. To this end it will be as untheatrical as possible. The play will be only "un prétexte, d'un ton un peu baroque" (PBQ. 93) and the action will be "éteinte dès le lever du rideau" (PBQ. 83). The real interest will reside in the characters and their situation. Antoine summarizes this situation. A man has just died. On the day of his funeral all the characters in his life meet after the burial for the traditional meal in his house. They take stock of his life and their own. That is all. The title of this play will be *Cher Antoine ou l'amour raté*. The actors Antoine has hired are, needless to say, the same as those who play his friends in the real *Cher Antoine*.

The object of this exercise is to break through the wall of egoism and theatrical hypocrisy which isolates people from each other in real life. Antoine hopes that the characters of his own life, in the guise of these actors and under his direction, will at last speak the "true text" of life, that which is never spoken in reality. This attempt fails, however, and the fault lies with Antoine himself. He miscasts his little play. The actor who plays Marcellin, Antoine's gentle doctor friend in the real *Cher Antoine*, is given the part of his acerbic and envious critic Cravatar. He is very obviously ill at ease in this part. Conversely, the actor who plays Cravatar in the real play is given the role of Marcellin here and he too is clearly temperamentally unsuited to it. When Antoine spots his "énorme erreur de distribution" (PBQ. 117) he realizes that he as dramatist is hampered by that same egocentric isolation he is trying to penetrate in others:

Ce n'était pas vous qui parliez, c'était vous, *vus par moi*. On n'en sort pas! On est en cage. On ne connaît les autres que par l'idée qu'on se fait d'eux. (PBQ. 112)

The obstacle lies in the dramatist himself, so Antoine tries another approach. He will retire entirely from the proceedings and allow his actors to improvise the scene he has outlined, just like in the avant-garde theatre. Antoine stretches out—dead—and the horrified actors do their best to improvise. But all they can produce is the same disjointed and aimless banalities and platitudes we hear in real life. Even this approach cannot penetrate the surface of life and get at the *pièce secrète* beneath.

In *Cher Antoine* Anouilh takes the same wide view of innovation and the Avant-garde as in *La Grotte*. This view is defined succinctly by Bachman in *Ne réveillez pas Madame* when he dismisses the young generation of playwrights as "déjà les vieux de quelqu'un" (PBQ. 236). The period setting of *Cher Antoine* is crucial in this respect. It takes place in 1913, a time when the first avant-garde movements of our century were already sweeping away the well-made plays of the nineteenth. We feel the ironic effect of this period setting when Cravatar contrasts Antoine's traditional, outmoded style to the thrust of the new Avant-garde:

Depuis l'évolution des esprits, la jeunesse . . . Il y a un muscle, un sang nouveau, voyez Bataille, le petit Bernstein! Tout bouge. (PBQ. 25)

This underlines the truth of Bachman's remark. Bataille and Bernstein are the predecessors of the modern generation and seem as outdated to contemporary playwrights as Antoine's work does to Cravatar. The same irony also affects Antoine's abortive play. Antoine has a great admiration for the new Russian theatre of his day, which Cravatar dismisses as "cette prétention nouvelle de faire des scènes avec des banalités" (PBQ. 83). But such an untheatrical style suits Antoine's purposes to perfection and it is on this he models his own project, which again Cravator recognizes as "une sorte de pièce russe comme on essaie de nous en vendre en ce moment" (PBQ. 83). Anouilh shares Antoine's fondness for Chekhov[1] and *Cher Antoine* borrows the ending of *The Cherry Orchard* which Antoine greatly admires. The last of the characters are leaving and Antoine's old house is being boarded up. As the shutters are nailed shut one by one, darkness gathers inside and the sound of hammering punctuates the last lines of the play. When all have gone and the house is dark and silent, their ghostly voices are heard

[1] *Arts*, Oct. 14th 1959.

echoing snatches of dialogue from the preceding scene. There is a long moment of silence on an empty stage and the curtain falls. But all this is too obviously 'theatrical'. This new style, banal, understated and untheatrical in the conventional sense, may have been revolutionary in its day and the opposite of all the well-made play stood for. But for a contemporary audience it is just as recognizable a style of theatre as any other. Despite his admiration for this ending, Antoine realized that "pour la resservir, il faudrait trouver un truc de théâtre" (PBQ. 133). Anouilh has found one, but the *pièce secrète* of life is no nearer in the end than it was in the beginning.

Cher Antoine, in its period setting and dramatic form, straddles a transitional period in theatre history, from the traditional well-made plays of the nineteenth century to the first avant-garde movements of our own age. Yet nothing has changed because every innovation, from the moment it is conceived, instantly becomes a theatrical style, subject to the same process of fossilization as that which it has replaced: And no recognizable theatrical style can reveal the untheatrical *pièce secrète* of life. The theatre, moreover, like life, changes less than it appears to. Beneath the superficial alterations in style and approach its essential themes remain unchanged. They revolve around the same family situation and basic, formative complexes which have preoccupied mankind in literature or in life, throughout history. This is illustrated in *Tu étais si gentil quand tu étais petit*. Based on the Orestes story, it was badly received by the critics, who felt that Anouilh had completely debased his subject. The play is based on the *Choephori* of Aeschylus and Anouilh even uses sections of dialogue from the standard French edition of Aeschylus.[1] It appears even so to be an unhappy and ill-judged hotch-potch of disparate elements. The ancient tragedy is performed as a play-within-the-play. The set is neutral and abstracted, incorporating a vaguely Grecian doorway, a stone bench and a tombstone. Orestes and Electra, in shapeless, timeless garb, play opposite an Aegisthus and Clytemnestra in Shakespearian costume. Downstage, a quartet of musicians in modern evening wear play in the intervals, comment on the action, gossip and discuss their own petty worries of the day.

The debasement of the Orestes myth is calculated for a purpose. It is designed to bring the ancient tragic myth down to earth and into the modern world. When the prestige of ancient tragedy is thus removed the story can be seen for what it is in essence—the same

[1] P. Mazon's bilingual edition, *Eschyle: œuvres*, Paris, Les Belles Lettres, 1961.

kind of family drama which is common to the other plays of this period. If the moral of the play can be summed up in a few words, then it is this:

la vie, c'est un bastringue! Et la tragédie grecque, pareille! (PS. 42)

The tragedy of the Atrides is no different in essence from the troubles besetting the modern bourgeois family. In keeping with this the values of the Greek original are replaced in Anouilh's version by the primal family complexes of modern bourgeois psychological drama. This is clearest in his treatment of Electra. In Anouilh's version she is a vengeful child who, because of her mother's crime, has never achieved normal emotional maturity and wishes to destroy the mother who destroyed the order, security and happiness of her childhood:

Sa mère elle-même a fait du cœur d'Électre un loup carnassier que rien jamais n'apaisera. (PS. 45)

By the same token, *Tu étais si gentil quand tu étais petit* creates a long perspective on man's preoccupations in the theatre. Julien in *Ne réveillez pas Madame* is haunted by the wish to stage one particular play, *Hamlet*, and dreams of acting out one scene in particular, that between Hamlet and his mother Gertrude in which he begs her:

Good night, but go not to my uncle's bed,
Assume a virtue if you have it not.[1]

This is the scene which, in Julien's eyes, enshrines the unhappy, neglected child's age-old plea for its mother's undivided attention and affection. It is no idle whim on Anouilh's part to have costumed Égisthe and Clytemnestre in *Tu étais si gentil quand tu étais petit* as a Shakespearian king and queen. Man, in the theatre as in life, has been preoccupied from time immemorial with the same fundamental problems and basic, recurring situation, from ancient Greek theatre, through Elizabethan theatre, to the modern day. The names may change but in the *pièce secrète* of life there are four or five permanent characters and the situation remains eternally the same.

Despite this wide, almost resigned, view of innovation in the theatre, Anouilh still stresses the importance of *métier* in these plays. In the preface to *Le Directeur de L'Opéra*, he writes:

Il n'y a que les métiers de vrai, et eux, on peut tenter de les réussir.

Antonio is no more successful at managing his job than his family

[1] *Hamlet*, Act III, sc. iv.

but he takes each day as it comes and does not give in to despair. In the same preface Anouilh analyses his character:

> il a du courage — qui reste, tous comptes faits, la seule vertu — il reconstruit le monde tous les matins, quitte à le voir s'effondrer tous les soirs avec une certaine naïveté de petit garçon, qui est probablement un de ses charmes . . . Il pense qu'il faut toujours tenter quelque chose et qu'en somme, le destin est distrait.

Anouilh has followed the example of Antonio in not giving up his own constant struggle over the years to improve his theatre. But questioned about his innovations in *Le Boulanger* the first play to break his silence after *La Grotte*, he was cautious about acknowledging any avant-garde mentality:

> L'avant-garde, n'est-ce pas, est toujours semblable à soi-même. Elle ne devient jamais classique. Elle est toujours ce qu'elle est . . . A vrai dire, c'est une disposition d'esprit, du moins à mon avis. Il me semble que cela n'est pas nécessaire pour apporter un son nouveau.[1]

In *Le Boulanger*, as in *Ne réveillez pas Madame, Les Poissons rouges, Cher Antoine, L'Arrestation*, Anouilh uses a fluid staging technique similar to that of *L'Alouette* and *Becket*. Like the historical plays, it is often a theatre-in-the-mind. Anouilh dramatizes on stage the memories and fantasies of his characters, without always taking the trouble to indicate that these are dream or fantasy sequences. This can be momentarily confusing but it is meant to make a point: the extent to which we depend on fantasy in our real lives and how, in extreme cases, it is difficult to distinguish real from imaginary. *Le Boulanger*, for example, is from the outset such an indistinguishable mixture of reality and fantasy. The play opens with an early morning dispute between Adolphe in his bath and Élodie at her dressing table. As Adolphe takes his shower and Élodie is dressing, her lover Adonard appears for a brief amorous episode. Adolphe seems completely unaware of Adonard's presence and for a good reason—he is a figment of Élodie's imagination. The whole play continues in a similar fashion. Chance remarks evoke instant fantasies which are immediately acted out and woven into the fabric of their daily lives. Illusion supplants reality in the end when in one of Toto's fantasies his parents are shot through the back of the head by Adolphe's boss and a band of marauding Indians. Toto is rescued by a young cavalry lieutenant and goes off to a new life—fighting Indians and learning to tie knots.

In fact, we can see in this technique a debt to Surrealism of

[1] *Les Nouvelles Littéraires*, loc. cit.

which, in Anouilh's opinion, "l'influence secrète se sent partout".[1] The use of daydreams and automatic association of ideas recalls the Surrealists' attempts to transcend everyday reality by exploring the relationship of the conscious and unconscious minds. The prominence given to mankind's primal complexes reflects the Surrealists' interest in Freudian psychology and *latent content* in art. The time theme and the non-chronological presentation of the action in these plays also recalls Surrealist attempts to reflect the unconscious mind's illogicality in the organization of the work of art.

Anouilh was typically cautious about this influence. He rejects the term Surrealism altogether in favour of the more non-committal word, 'fantasy' which man has used from time immemorial to escape from and compensate for the deceptions of real living.[2] That is exactly what he is illustrating in these plays. He regards Surrealism, moreover, as only one more manifestation of an age-old wish to represent the flow of human consciousness.[3] Anouilh came into contact with Surrealism through Roger Vitrac, whose influence has already been discussed in Chapter Five. Anouilh did homage to his dead friend by producing a successful adaptation of *Victor ou les enfants au pouvoir* in 1963. This renewed contact with Vitrac's work obviously influenced his choice of a new style. Even so, it is significant that Anouilh regards Vitrac as having grafted Surrealist ideas and techniques on to a much older tradition of French comic theatre.[4]

Anouilh has not abandoned that tradition in these latest plays but rather done what he sees in Vitrac—grafted his new style on to it. *Le Boulanger*, as Anouilh indicates in his programme note, "se joue presque intégralement en caleçons et en chemise, comme un Feydeau". Despite the open plan, impressionistic sets, use of blackouts and mixture of real and imaginary, *Le Boulanger* has its roots in vaudeville and Anouilh hopes that "on rira souvent". The same is true of the other plays in this chapter, all of which are written in Anouilh's now permanent tragic-comic mode. Even *Tu étais si gentil quand tu étais petit*, despite the Greek tragedy at its core, has a comic element, assured by the presence of the quartet and their amusing, if earthy, reflections on life, love and Greek tragedy. The tone is often grating or grotesque but the invitation is still to laugh at life rather than cry.

The criticisms levelled at Anouilh over the years for his taste for

[1] *Le Figaro Littéraire*, Oct. 6th 1962.
[2] Vandromme, op. cit., p. 171.
[3] Archer, op. cit., p. 44.
[4] Vandromme, loc. cit., *Le Figaro Littéraire*, loc. cit.

music hall jokes, outdated comedy and general facility in his approach to the theatre surface in these plays. Among the many recriminations of Antoine's wife in *Les Poissons rouges* is:

> Popescu, lui, fait rire par l'absurde. Ton comique à toi, est dépassé. Nous ne nous sentons plus concernés. Tu ne pourrais pas te pénétrer un peu du tragique et de l'absurdité de la condition humaine, non? Cela serait trop pour toi? Un homme de cœur le ferait—au moins pour sa famille! Mais non! Toi, tu mets ton point d'honneur à ne pas être dans le vent! (NPG. 463)

Anouilh's riposte is to ennoble his professional man of the theatre in the person of Antoine de Saint-Flour. The artist is an aristocrat, in Anouilh's view, by virtue of his talents which are bestowed on him at birth and not acquired by study. Anouilh's aristocratic dramatists have inherited "cette très ancienne habitude de parler légèrement — de penser légèrement — de tout" (NPG. 579).

The ability to laugh at life's absurdity is a very ancient gift—embodied in that old comic tradition from which Anouilh draws his inspiration. If this instinct has not been conferred on an individual at birth it cannot be acquired by effort and intelligence alone. Anouilh feels that modern man, in pursuit of greater equality, has lost his native nobility—that is, the power and courage to laugh at his own eternal absurdity and at the horror and misery of the human condition. Anouilh has made it the aim and justification of his long career in the theatre to restore to the twentieth century that ability to face life with poise and facility, in which reside the real dignity and the truly aristocratic spirit of man.

Conclusion

Jean Anouilh can justly claim to be an *homme de théâtre*. Outside the theatre he has to his credit one long-forgotten short story published in 1939, *L'Histoire de Monsieur Mauvette et de la fin du monde*[1] and a book of modern fables, some based on La Fontaine, some original, written in 1961.[2] Apart from occasional articles for newspapers, magazines and periodicals, the rest of his energies have been devoted to theatrical writing of one kind or another. His collected plays to date total nine volumes and these do not yet include his most recent works and several shorter pieces. He also has to his credit a few television scripts and a fair number of film scenarios and adaptations for the stage of other people's work. From the beginning he has taken a close interest in the production of his plays and has been collaborating on them officially since the sixties.

Anouilh's most recent plays are not perhaps among his best, but some unevenness is only to be expected over such a long, active and prolific career. More remarkable is the consistently high general standard of craftsmanship Anouilh has maintained over the years. There are very fine plays in every period of his work and, of the more recent ones, both *Ne réveillez pas Madame* and *Cher Antoine* were nominated for awards by the drama critics. Relations with his critics have not always been so affable but he has remained a firm favourite with actors and other theatre people who find his plays eminently 'playable'. This is no doubt a welcome accolade for a man who regards himself primarily as a theatrical craftsman and who only departs from his usual reticence and modesty to claim this honour:

Je suis un ouvrier de théâtre. Le côté artisanal du théâtre me ravit.[3]

Anouilh probably inherited his artistic temperament and love of the theatre from his musician mother but his father's side of the family contributed something equally important. Anouilh's grand-

[1] *Cahiers de la Compagnie Renaud–Barrault*, vol. 26, May 1959.
[2] La Table Ronde, 1962.
[3] *Carrefour*, March 1st 1961.

father was a gentleman's tailor in Bordeaux. Anouilh's father carried on the craft and the business until, in the aftermath of the First World War, he was obliged to sell up, move to Paris and take a job as a tailor's cutter.[1] From his father Anouilh inherited his high standards and a sense of pride in his *métier*:

> Mon père était coupeur-tailleur. C'était un homme fin et simple, et qui connaissait merveilleusement son métier. Il en avait la fierté et les exigences. «Tournant mal» dans la littérature, j'ai toujours rêvé d'être aussi bon artisan que lui . . . Sans fausse honte, j'ai, comme on dit, un métier dans les mains.[2]

It is interesting that the *métier* theme in Anouilh's writing—the value of accepting one's allotted task and the humble pride of doing it to the best of one's abilities—comes to the fore in the mid-forties at a time when the idealistic values of his first period are being undermined. Pride in his craft has become an important part of Anouilh's ethics over the years:

> Mon père avait le goût de son métier qui est un art. J'ai vraiment eu avec lui le sentiment de la conscience professionnelle, de la noblesse que cela donne à un homme.[3]

Ironically, his critics have turned this pride against him, riposting that, having found a commercially successful formula of popular comedy, he has been unable or unwilling to forsake it. The three pillars of this criticism are his fidelity over the years to a number of constant themes, characters and situations; his refusal to treat seriously or at all what some consider to be the great burning issues of today; his acquiescence in a relatively traditional dramatic format along with a deplorable penchant for theatrical clichés and conventions, old music hall jokes and *mots d'auteur*.

The charge of repetitiveness is nothing new. As early as 1938 Anouilh was explaining:

> Nous avons tous un ou deux problèmes qui nous intéressent particulièrement et auxquels on se tient. On cherche à résoudre de petits problèmes qui vous ont frappés. Les pièces finissent par avoir un air de famille.[4]

This family resemblance has grown more pronounced since but to use it as a criticism is rather shortsighted. Every writer has a nucleus of preoccupations from which his creative impulse stems

[1] *Paris-Match*, Oct. 21st 1972.
[2] *Opéra*, March 7th 1951.
[3] *Paris-Match*, loc. cit.
[4] *Le Figaro*, Jan. 11th 1938.

and there is no writer with a personal and sincere vision of life who could not be 'reduced' to a number of characteristic themes. We should be even more circumspect in Anouilh's case when he has clearly been fostering resemblances by self-quotation, self-plagiarism and even self-parody on occasion. It is almost as if he were creating a modern Commedia dell'Arte in which familiar figures reappear, sometimes without even a change of name, in variations on a given scenario. If this is slightly overstated, at least it indicates an underlying cohesion in his dramatic universe which suggests he has not "deviated from his profoundest intentions".[1]

It is hardly an exaggeration to say that there is only one central theme running through the whole of Anouilh's work—the eternal and universal conflict between idealism and reality. All his other themes are related to this, either as expressions of the idealistic rejection of life or as explorations of the various obstacles to idealism and self-realization in an imperfect world. In the plays of the thirties and forties we find a direct conflict between the intense, idealistic expectations of Anouilh's "heroic race" and the pedestrian *bonheur* and inevitable compromises of life. In the fifties it is still the same theme which is debated in terms of *rigueur* and *facilité*. Anouilh's earlier idealism is caricatured in the *rigueur* of Julien in *Colombe* or of Ludovic in *L'Hurluberlu*, but there is also an undercurrent of poignant nostalgia for earlier times. Those characters, especially the dramatist-heroes of the fifties and sixties who play at life with deliberate *facilité*, do so because they are at heart disillusioned idealists. As his heroes age, marital love and family life naturally loom larger in the plays, but still we have not forsaken the central theme. True love in Anouilh is a glimpse of an ideal state which by definition cannot endure. His couples' mutual recriminations over dead love and fading desire are one more instance of the degradation of all ideals in an imperfect world.

This is not to say, however, that Anouilh's preoccupations, while remaining constant, have not matured. On the contrary, Anouilh's attitudes and sympathies have altered significantly over the years. Looking back on his career in 1967, after his silence in the early sixties, Anouilh remarked:

J'ai l'impression que toutes mes anciennes pièces ont été écrites par mon père . . . Il est vrai qu'Antigone m'agace. Ses grandes souffrances seraient insupportables si elle n'était une enfant.[2]

[1] P. H. Simon, *Théâtre et Destin*, p. 144; cf. also Introduction, p. 7.
[2] *L'Express*, Oct. 9th 1967.

In fact, there is no better illustration of both his consistency and maturation than the childhood theme. In the plays of his first period childhood is, implicitly or explicitly, a time of sheltered innocence into which one may escape from the realities of adult life, as in *Le Voyageur sans bagage*, or by which one may measure the deceptions of growing up, as in *Antigone*. After *L'Invitation au château* the view of childhood innocence changes radically. In *Ardèle* and *La Valse des Toréadors*, the later *L'Hurluberlu* and, most recently, in *Chers Zoiseaux*, Anouilh's youngsters are sexually precocious and adept at imitating their elders' more unpleasant habits. In the works of the sixties and seventies as a whole, childhood, far from being a haven of innocence, security and happiness, is a traumatic time and the source of all adult discontent and hence many of society's ills. There was a childish or childlike quality about the stubborn intransigence of Anouilh's former heroes and heroines, which set them apart. Now the whole of adult society stands accused of immaturity and infantilism. Childhood has, then, remained one of that nucleus of characteristic themes throughout the plays, becoming, if anything, even more central to Anouilh's view of his fellow man. The perspective has, however, changed substantially.

This re-emphasis of the importance of childhood in Anouilh's view of society is paralleled in the evolution of his dramatic form. We remember that his earliest contacts with the theatre were as a child in Arcachon, the popular resort on the coast near his native Bordeaux. To supplement the family income his mother put her musical abilities to use, playing in café orchestras during the year and doing the summer season in the orchestra of the Casino d'Arcachon. As the pianist's son, Anouilh was allowed in to see the summer productions.[1] It can be no coincidence that café orchestras and musical ensembles figure in several plays and that some of his musicians boast of the—dubious—distinction of having won second prize at the Conservatoire d'Arcachon. *L'Arrestation* is the most interesting play in this respect. Although by no means autobiographical, it is the most suggestive of Anouilh's childhood contact with Arcachon. The hero of this play returns to just such a resort as Arcachon where he used to spend the summer with his mother who was a member of the Casino orchestra. He finds everything a lot less grandiose and more tawdry than he remembers from childhood. In contrast, as Anouilh grows older, he emphasizes more and more the importance of his first impressions of the theatre. The kind of theatre it was is significant. The repertoire consisted, not of serious

[1] *Paris-Match*, loc. cit.

drama, but of turn-of-the-century operettas, the French equivalent of our own Gilbert and Sullivan. The colour, music, spectacle, innocent exaggeration and obvious artifice of this kind of theatre made a vivid and lasting impression:

> Je crois que cela a été mon premier choc au théâtre. Le fond de mon théâtre se trouve là. Il y a le comique, le trivial, le traître, le jeune premier. J'en suis resté au théâtre de mon enfance.[1]

This fondness for a traditional, outmoded style of theatre is equally a symptom or an expression of Anouilh's instinctively theatrical view of life which we have seen in even his earliest, serious plays. Just as some people are sensitive to light, noise or pollens in the air, so others are sensitive to the theatrical side of human behaviour. This is probably more of an affliction than an advantage. It seems to become progressively more pervasive to the point where nothing appears real or where what may be genuine also has a simultaneously theatrical side:

> au point que je vois les gens qui mentent: je ne peux plus aller à un enterrement sans me dire au milieu des lamentations, celle-là ment, mon Dieu qu'elle est mauvaise.[2]

This view may be personal but it is not arbitrary. Anouilh has demonstrated its validity down the years and, at the same time, justified his penchant for the poetic and conventionalized theatre of his childhood, both by his exploration of human behaviour and psychology and by the function he has evolved for his theatre.

In the first plays we can see a distinction between real and theatrical living. The main characters of Chapter One, Frantz, Marc and Thérèse, are presented as 'real' people, surrounded by lesser theatrical characters. When Anouilh embraces theatricalism in 1936 all his characters are henceforth presented as conscious or unconscious role-players and his plays give up any pretence at realism to concentrate on demonstrating and underlining their own artificiality. It is an integral part of his theatricalist approach that he toys with the conventions of his medium and plundering the repertoire of theatrical effects also contributes to the creation of an unreal, fantasy world into which he invites us to escape from everyday reality. His liking, for example, for "ce monde fascinant et pourri du théâtre de l'avant Première Guerre mondiale, que j'ai si souvent imaginé et tenté de faire vivre",[3] in which he sets several

[1] ibid.
[2] *Paris-Match*, June 13th 1959.
[3] Anouilh in preface to *La Traversée d'une vie* by Françoise Rosay.

plays, is all part of the effort to transpose real emotions into an unreal world and render them harmless and appropriate to the theatrical game of make-believe.

As Anouilh continues to explore the intricacies of role-playing in life his defence of his practice goes deeper. Even after his adoption of theatricalism it is still possible on occasion to see some distinction between theatre and some kind of reality. Antigone, for example, who begins by seeing herself playing the role of a heroine in a Greek tragedy, is disillusioned as the action progresses and brought to face the reality of her situation. The old gods are dead and she is alone in an absurd world with no absolute values. The cause in which she claims to be acting is inauthentic and her real motives are personal. Her initial vision of herself as an *héroïne de théâtre* is shattered, even if it is replaced by an equally theatrical reality—a vision of herself condemned to act out a role in which destiny has arbitrarily cast her in an absurd world. By the time we come to *L'Alouette* and *Becket*, even this theatrical reality has receded and it is now the characters' theatrical vision of themselves which is allowed to triumph. Whereas Antigone was made to see the inauthenticity of her cause, Joan and Becket do not suspect the ironies and ambiguities which undermine their claims to be acting in the name of a greater authority than themselves. They are dominated by their roles and, as in the case of Bitos, the roles in which they see themselves have supplanted true self-awareness.

This view of the human mind at work is the core of Anouilh's justification for his use of conventionalized forms in the theatre. If that image we have of our innermost selves is only an inauthentic, theatrical image of a real self which we do not know, then the possibility of discovering any ultimate truth about existence seems remote. In fact, Anouilh goes further by suggesting that we can only conceive of any such ultimate reality in conventionalized terms. In this lies both a defence of and a function for his own brand of *théâtre artificiel*. Writing in admiration of Shakespeare and Molière, and taking example from their transposition of life into conventionalized and poetic terms, Anouilh stated his conviction:

> L'homme ne peut connaître la vraie vie, qui est informe, qu'en lui donnant une forme. L'art du théâtre est de lui en donner une, aussi fausse, aussi arbitraire que possible et de faire plus vrai que le vrai.[1]

In other words, the play can only ever be a kind of façade or "un prétexte d'un ton un peu baroque" (PBQ. 93) for the real

[1] *Carrefour*, loc. cit.

play, the *pièce secrète* of life, which the dramatist cannot write. On the other hand, if what we think of as real life is only a theatrical image of an ultimately unknowable reality, then the dramatist can at least, by producing an even more artificial and conventionalized image of life in his plays, begin to suggest what lies beyond.

This apparently resigned and defeatist attitude should not be equated with a lack of artistic or social commitment. On the contrary, the history of Anouilh's development as an artist is, as we have seen, one of sustained self-scrutiny and criticism. He has always been anxious to define a function for his theatre and to reappraise his approach in keeping with that function and his maturing vision of life. If this self-renewal has led him, not to the more obviously experimental types of modern theatre, but back to a seemingly outmoded style of drama, that is because he has realized the limits and the futility of the Avant-garde. This is a vague designation which covers a multitude, but it is clear from the parody of avant-garde drama in *L'Hurluberlu* what Anouilh has in mind and why he takes issue with it.[1] This kind of theatre only captures the surface banalities of life and cannot, therefore, reveal or suggest either life's theatricality or the *vraie vie* which lies beneath:

> Il y a d'ailleurs des wagons de métro à six heures, des queues de guichet de gare où l'on fait . . . de très bon théâtre d'avant-garde.[2]

Moreover, as Antoine realized in *Cher Antoine*, all new approaches quickly degenerate into recognizable 'styles' with their own conventions and the Avant-garde is no exception:

> elle est à son poste, sentinelle semblable à elle-même, à un tic près, depuis 1920.[3]

When the first shock of novelty has passed, we are no nearer glimpsing *la vraie vie* than we were before. Even so, Anouilh's attitude to innovation is ambiguous. Despite his ultimate pessimism, he has not given up the struggle to improve his own work. But innovation, in his view, is relative and draws its real vitality from tradition:

> L'inspiration, ce n'est qu'une broderie sur des figures immuables.[4]

Those whom he admires as the greatest innovators in the modern theatre since Pirandello, for example Vitrac, Beckett, Ionesco and

[1] NPG. 89; cf. also ch. 7, p. 110.
[2] Vandromme, op. cit., p. 218.
[3] ibid., p. 217.
[4] *Arts*, Nov. 16th 1951.

Genet, he sees as having transcended the Avant-garde and grafted their preoccupations on to an older tradition:

They have come to the real theatre, leaving the Avant-garde where it always is.[1]

Although he has not himself produced as new a style as Beckett or Ionesco, Anouilh is none the less proud to be 'modern' in the broadest sense. By virtue of his rejection of realism and the well-made play, his theatricalism and his unflagging interest in the conventions of his medium, he includes himself in that broad movement in twentieth-century theatre which is descended from Pirandello:

nous sommes quelques-uns du métier qui travaillons depuis l'autre guerre à étrangler l'anecdote, à tuer la notion de «pièce bien faite», qui règne sur le théâtre français depuis Scribe . . . Pirandello, dans un coup de génie, dont on ne dira jamais assez l'importance, s'est donné un jour la peine de l'étrangler jusqu'à l'asphyxie complète avec *Six personnages*.[2]

Where he is unrepentantly less modern is in his refusal to commit himself to any political ideology, espouse any social cause or even discuss, as Camus and Sartre do for example, the philosophical principles behind political action:

Certains me disent démodé, en dehors du coup. On voudrait que je fasse des pièces-à-thèse, que j'expose de grands principes. Or, je n'arrive pas à me prendre assez au sérieux.[3]

Gilbert Mury made a point about Anouilh's first plays which remains valid for the whole of his work since. Mury remarked that, despite the lucid and sensitive expression of the effects of poverty on the individual, there is a noticeable absence of any commitment to social reform.[4] Anouilh himself added a revealing caveat at the time on the interpretation of *La Sauvage*:

Il y a une confusion surtout que je redoute. Vous connaissez mon sujet? Pourvu qu'on n'aille pas voir là une opposition de classes.[5]

As ever, this is not the whole story. We can find themes in Anouilh which are at least potentially socio-political, such as his long-standing interest in justice, which grows from passing references to prison conditions in the early plays to greater prominence in *Pauvre Bitos, Les Poissons rouges* and *Tu étais si gentil* . . . We

[1] *International Herald-Tribune*, Sept. 18th 1970.
[2] *Opéra*, loc. cit.
[3] *Tribune de Genève*, Dec. 12th 1966.
[4] G. Mury, *Les Intellectuels devant l'action*, pp. 29, 33.
[5] *Le Figaro*, loc. cit.

also recall how deeply Anouilh was affected by the Brasillach affair and the kind of justice meted out after the War. Yet none of this plunged him into politics, despite his "opposition sentimentale profonde"[1] to De Gaulle. Anouilh is not a political animal. He has his views, of course, but claims that these are instinctive and emotional rather than carefully reasoned out:

Je n'ai pas de pensées politiques. Mes refus restent des refus de concierge.[2]

However true that may be, Anouilh's interests do certainly lie with people and not abstract issues. If he is interested in justice it is as an expression of human nature and, in particular, of man's inhumanity to man. He views politics in the same perspective. In *Pauvre Bitos*, for example, his preoccupation is not with party politics but with man as a political animal:

la critique sociale ne m'intéresse pas. Il faut moquer l'homme, cela suffit.[3]

This is not Anouilh's way of opting out. A partisan writer will have some allies but when you reveal the absurdities of human behaviour in all fields and criticize all sides, attacking your fellow countrymen for their vindictiveness—"pour longtemps, la haine est française" (PG. 418)—or reproaching the whole of contemporary adult society for its immaturity—"enfantins comme nous sommes tous en train de le devenir"[4]—then you have few friends anywhere.

Charges of complacency against Anouilh are further diminished by the presence of that internal debate we have seen in his work between the form and the function of his theatre. There is a clear ethical need in Anouilh to justify his theatricalist approach to the drama and also the privileged lifestyle his talent has conferred on him. In the light of this ethical need it seems almost inevitable that Anouilh puts the dramatist himself on stage and surrounds him with the reproaches of family and friends, colleagues and critics. It is one more development in an unrelenting process of self-criticism. The answer to this need for self-justification comes from commitment, but commitment in a wider and more circumspect sense than its usual social or political connotations. Horace has defined it in *L'Invitation au château*:

Il faut se laisser gouverner . . . Attacher trop d'importance à l'argent qu'on vous prend ou aux gestes qu'on fait exiger de vous, dans la rue, par les gendarmes, c'est l'attitude la plus futile, la plus inconsidérée qui soit.

[1] *Paris-Match*, Oct. 21st 1972.
[2] ibid.
[3] *Le Figaro Littéraire*, Oct. 6th 1963.
[4] Programme note to *Le Boulanger*.

Mais permettre au destin de vous conduire . . . c'est impardonnable." (PB. 40)

Many would disagree violently with Anouilh on the futility of political commitment but his argument is that all other restrictions on men, social, political or economic, pale into insignificance beside the greatest oppression of all—the inevitability of death in an absurd world. Helping to remedy this 'injustice', which afflicts all men equally, is, in Anouilh's view, the proper concern and function of the writer. In fact, Anouilh would probably shrink from such generalizations but this is the background to his own proud assertion that he is a humble craftsman of the theatre, providing employment for actors and an opportunity for the public to escape from themselves and their worries for the space of an evening.[1] This view of the theatre's function in turn elevates Anouilh's incorrigible lack of *sérieux* in the theatre to something more deliberate and purposeful. The dramatic form he has evolved has its roots in an age-old comic tradition which, as he indicates, goes back at least as far as the Atellan farces of ancient Rome.[2] This comic tradition is not trivial and escapist. On the contrary, it is positive in Anouilh's eyes because mankind has used it from time immemorial as a means of facing the harsh realities of existence and defending itself against them by transposing them into comic terms and laughing at them:

Grâce à Molière, le vrai théâtre français est le seul où on ne dise pas la messe, mais où on rit, comme des hommes à la guerre . . . de notre misère et de notre horreur.[3]

Anouilh's debt to this comic tradition places his anti-intellectualism on a more reasonable basis. Two things have become associated in his mind. One is the growing democratization of modern society and the other the contemporary tendency to despair and to take a tragic view of life. They are related because democracy and, especially, the spread of education have increased both the number and the influence of intellectuals in present-day society. It is they who "découvrent périodiquement et un peu ingénument l'horreur de la condition humaine et qui voudraient nous empêcher de nous divertir au théâtre"[4] Anouilh, by dipping into an ancient and unintellectual tradition of comic theatre, is inviting us to do the opposite—not to despair at our misery but to laugh at our absurdity.

The comic dramatist is, in Anouilh's estimation, an aristocrat in

[1] *International Herald-Tribune*, loc. cit.; *L'Avant-Scène*, Dec. 15th 1959.
[2] *L'Avant-Scène*, May 15th 1974; cf. also ch. 5, p. 75.
[3] Vandromme, op. cit., p. 143.
[4] ibid.

an increasingly egalitarian age because he has inherited at birth this gift of being able to laugh at himself and of not taking life seriously which cannot be acquired by any amount of study, personal merit or intellectual prowess:

La généralisation de la culture va certainement multiplier, dans les temps à venir, le nombre déjà important des ouvriers de la pensée . . . le nombre des auteurs comiques ne changera pas.[1]

Anouilh's anti-intellectualism does not contradict his view of the theatre as a *jeu de l'esprit*. The safest translation of this phrase might be 'game of the imagination' and not of the 'mind' or 'intellect'. He warns against any confusion:

On vient au théâtre pour jouer au jeu de l'esprit (ce qui ne veut pas dire du tout, au jeu d'intellectuel).[2]

The distinction is valid because the comic theatre has no need of intellectual or rational analysis in order to get its message across. In his preface to a volume of Labiche's plays Anouilh explains how the comic theatre works. Taking Molière as his example, he writes:

La force explosive d'une réplique a produit le même effet destructif qu'un chapitre de Montaigne; en moins d'une seconde dans un éclair, nous avons su — tout su — sur l'homme et nous avons ri. Mais ni Molière . . . ni nous n'avons *pensé* pendant ce très court et violent phénomène.[3]

This preface is also interesting for Anouilh's view of Labiche's place in the nineteenth-century theatre. One comes away with the distinct impression that Anouilh is comparing it to his own in the twentieth. Labiche was a "petit bourgeois tranquille" who excelled in the minor genre of light comedy. He produced no grand theories on his art but applied himself competently and methodically to making audiences laugh and earning as much money as possible in the process. The audiences of the 1850s and 60s no doubt felt that the great and enduring drama of the age was being written by Augier and Alexandre Dumas *fils*. Yet Labiche's gift for making people laugh at themselves ensures that he is still enjoyed today when Augier and Dumas are gathering dust on library shelves. Anouilh is nothing if not a modest man:

Je ne vise ni la postérité . . . ni le respect de mes contemporains. Je n'écris que pour m'amuser.[4]

[1] Anouilh in *Le Mystère Labiche*, *Œuvres Complètes de Labiche*, vol. 5.
[2] *Jour*, March 12th 1935.
[3] *Le Mystère Labiche*, loc. cit.
[4] *Arts*, Oct. 14th 1959.

Whether or not his modesty is justified only time will tell; but the chances are high that audiences will still be laughing at Anouilh when the Augiers and the Dumas of our own century have been forgotten.

Appendix I

English Texts of French Quotations

Introduction

7. 'I have been working in the theatre for a fair number of years now and with enough success for it to appear suspect to some.'
   'Jean Anouilh has fallen into the trap which lies in wait for the all too gifted writer. There comes a moment when mastery of his medium damages the density of his message. The impetus of creative emotion is replaced by the search for stylistic effects and brilliance of style degenerates finally into a gratuitous automatism ungoverned by the dictates of his thought. Having stated the essentials in the works of his youth and early maturity, a cunning and resourceful writer, accustomed to applause, forsakes his deepest intentions for circumstantial interests, sometimes political in nature, in order to elicit laughter through satire or allusion.'
11. 'old entertainer, bashful and far from candid'
    'With Jean Anouilh, there are never any theories on theatre.'
12. 'I have no biography.'
    'I have given myself entirely to my art and have reflected at length upon it. I here gather together my partisan reflections.'
13. 'certain things which the professional critic is perhaps less well placed to know and see.'

Chapter One

14. 'The ability to be happy is not given to all.'
    'plays of a familiar kind'
16. 'constructed for an act and not around an action.'
17. 'You disgust me, all of you, with your talk of happiness. You would think that nothing else mattered in the world. Well I, yes I, want to flee from it." (PN. 207)
    'and I have all my life before me to be happy.' (PN. 235)
    'the drama is a mixture of tragedy and comedy' (PN. 118)
18. 'I reworked the play several times; it came to life, you might say, in concentric layers.'
19. '*Looking towards the drawing room where Florent is playing, as if she still had many things to tell him, she murmurs*: 'You know . . .' *But she turns away sharply and disappears into the night. Only her wedding dress remains, shining white in the darkness.*' (PN. 273)
    'where, by repeated cuts, we finally left Ludmilla nothing to say but a long silence, which she said so well . . .'

20. 'I would never have written *La Sauvage* had I not known what it meant to be poor. It is through someone else that I really came to know poverty: this someone was my first wife, Monelle Valentin . . . who had had a truly wretched childhood.'
'obsessional, haunted theatre'
21. 'THÉRÈSE: Until just now – it's strange – I did not know. I was innocent. It's they who have just taught me that also.
FLORENT: What?
THÉRÈSE: What I was, what you were.' (PN. 177)
'that an act is not only what it is, but also what it seems to be.'
'You know nothing about being human, Florent.' (PN. 221)
23. 'I do not think that the work stands up to scrutiny.'

Chapter Two

24. 'It seems to me that it is all in *Le Bal des Voleurs*; my characters and my themes.'
25. 'plots are being hatched, marriages prepared. Personally, I cannot follow them. They bring on my migraine.' (PR. 41)
'I never understand a thing and, above all, they bore me.' (PR. 42)
26. 'For sixty years, I believed that life had to be taken seriously. That is far too much. I feel like committing a great folly.' (PR. 43)
'And, what is graver still, I realise that between the little girl I was and the old woman I am, there has been nothing, beneath all the fuss, but an even greater loneliness.
EVA: I thought you were happy.
LADY HURF: You haven't got good eyes. I am playing a role. I play it well like everything I do, that's all . . . (PR. 65)
27. 'I play with fire and the fire will not even burn me.' (PR. 65)
'Only for those who played it with all their youth has the pretence succeeded, and then only because they staked their youth, which always succeeds.' (PR. 130)
'My little Juliette will be saved because she is romantic and simple. It is a grace not given to us all.' (PR. 65)
'I wrote *Le Bal des Voleurs* resolutely. I am very proud of the laughter which punctuates its performance each evening at the Atelier theatre, and I would not think more highly of myself for having written a drawing-room comedy full of allusions or an illustrated lesson in political economy.'
28. 'a story does not necessarily have to be treated in all its naive rigour or natural simplicity and primitiveness: the dramatist can and must play with his characters, their passions and their intrigues.'
'my helplessness in the face of the world . . . a world which one cannot enter.'
'coffee-and-croissants existence, of bohemian poverty'

'bohemian, but not tragic, poverty'

'I have never had the impression of being poor, even if I was. I have always had the impression of being rich.'

29. 'Its success worried me a little. I wondered if it was entirely sound. But its success also encouraged me since I was no longer interested in the theatre.'

'A theatrical performance is a game which obeys precise rules. We must accept its conventions, 'conventions' here meaning 'the rules of the game'.

30. 'and then suddenly, I had the idea of lengthening it'

'My enthusiasm is returning now that I know it is possible to create an artificial theatre.'

'No doubt I am the only man in effect to whom destiny will have given the chance of accomplishing what everyone dreams of . . .' (PN. 371)

31. '*Le Voyageur sans bagage* is to Anouilh's other plays what a laboratory experiment is to a natural phenomenon.'

34. 'which opens by itself as in murder mysteries' (PR. 182)

'Ah! so there you are? You have arrived in time. The atmosphere is just right. It's exactly the moment for theatrical apparitions. We are in the thick of mystery and suspense . . . It's the 'Mysteries of New York' all over again, with the pale, delicate heroine dragged trembling by Monsieur into the darkest of adventures.' (PR. 222)

'As for the main character, he does not have to be analysed: his personality consists in not having any . . .'

'*I* exist, despite all your stories' (PN. 352)

36. 'the charms of creative liberty'

37. 'he had such a bad character. Amnesia or not, why should he not still have it?' (PN. 361)

'Ah no, maître . . . Something tells me that Gaston is going to recognize this Renaud family as his own; that he will rediscover in this house the atmosphere of his past. Something tells me that it is here he will recover his memory. It is a woman's instinct which has rarely let me down.' (PN. 280)

38. 'the play advances in retrograde fashion'

'The construction of Anouilh's play borders on paradox, containing but one positive action, envisaged but not accomplished three lines from the end.'

'even one's humblest gestures can only be the prolongation of earlier gestures' (PN. 365)

'do violence to nature'

'These characters exist. These characters are already half alive. Someone believes in them. Someone expects from them certain words, certain gestures . . .' (PR. 165)

39. 'to bring imaginary characters to life' (PR. 165)

'You knew that the theatre is first and foremost a matter of

CHARACTERS'
'It is the audience alone which gives it its equilibrium and its necessity.'
'to make people believe in a fleeting reality'

40. 'I am doing all this quite simply because I am forgetting, Mademoiselle.' (PR. 330)
    '*The Prince sighs in spite of himself*: Léocadia . . .
    Amanda, softly, as if it were she: Yes my love. Put your hands on my hips . . .' (PR. 371)
    'haze of boredom from which I thought I would never emerge.' (PR. 354)
    'She was intelligence itself' (PR. 354)
41. 'I believe simply that, fleeing realism with its narrow psychology, its tears and eternal situations, it must be possible to play in one way or another with a subject instead of submitting to it.'

Chapter Three

46. 'You disgust me, all of you, with your happiness! With your life that must be loved, come what may . . . *I* want everything now, in its entirety, or else I refuse! . . . I want to be sure of everything today and I want it all to be as beautiful as when I was little – or else I want to die.' (NPN. 188)
51. 'Now the spring is coiled. It has only to unwind of its own accord. That is the advantage of tragedy, a little push sets things in motion . . . Afterwards, you need only let them take their course. No need to worry. The mechanism functions by itself. It is meticulous and well-oiled, and has been from time immemorial." (NPN. 160, 161)
52. 'dying becomes terrifying, like an accident' (NPN. 161)
    'It might have been possible to escape . . .' (NPN. 161)
53. 'those who remain unburied wander eternally and never find rest' (NPN. 169)
    'two thieves who fell out among themselves while deceiving us and cut each other's throats like the two little thugs they were.' (NPN. 184)
    'For no one. For myself.' (NPN. 174)
54. 'tête à tête with destiny and death' (NPN. 170)
56. 'Peculiar weather for an idyll' (NPN. 302)
57. 'No one will ever pity you . . . the man Jason judges you along with the rest of men.' (NPN. 382)
    'I did however have something to say' (NPN. 398)
    'There will be bread again for everyone this year.' (NPN. 399)
    'The world had a form before, be it good or bad.' (NPN. 339)
    'This world, this chaos through which you led me by the hand, I want it to take on a shape at last.' (NPN. 388)

58. 'poor, man-made scaffolding' (NPN. 388)
'flimsy wall, built by my hands between the absurd nothingness of existence and myself' (NPN. 390)

Chapter Four

59. 'Unable to remedy death, misery and ignorance, mankind has decided, in order to be happy, simply not to think about them.'
'One cheats death by preventing people thinking about themselves.'
'I shall stop writing altogether for two years. I shall abandon my characters to their own devices and look for a new way for my theatre.'
'who corresponds best today to Anouilh's own preoccupations'
'a time when France behaved ignobly'
60. 'Brasillach's death overwhelmed me'
'I was very pure at thirty: rigour still meant something to me then'
'The young man that I was and the young man Brasillach died the same day and – relatively speaking – of the same thing.'
62. 'We are quite alone, that much is certain. We can do nothing for each other but play the game.' (PB. 126)
'the worst of theatrical conventions' (PB. 39)
63. 'Things were divided out between us. He got all the heart, I got something else.' (PB. 72)
'He is very intelligent, much more than I am. Very courageous too, very intrepid.' (PB. 69)
'We are too negligent . . . I can understand that in politics. We must accept being governed like we accept having our hair cut – by someone else – after a fashion . . . But to allow yourself to be led by destiny, that is serious, mademoiselle, that is unforgiveable . . . I do not feel in a mood for tolerating the normal order of things today. Well, so much the worse for fatality . . . I am taking responsibility for everything and shuffling the cards.' (PB. 40, 41)
64. 'I love no one, mademoiselle. That is what will allow me to organise this evening's little entertainment with complete detachment.' (PB. 40)
'the successful caricature of their own ostentation.' (PB. 100)
'old ladies . . . who are beginning to see things clearly' (PB. 145)
'Everything must end happily; that is traditional.' (PB. 152)
'a vague nostalgia for the swish of red velvet curtains'
65. 'MADAME DESMERMORTES: So here we are again, both of us, feeling very silly and not even sure if we have acted for the best.
HORACE: For the best, for the worst? . . . Are you still at that stage? You surprise me, aunt. I thought you much more positive than that.' (PB. 133)
'One is never all that handsome, mademoiselle, without being very human at the same time. It is not everything to have nice eyes. There

must be a little lamp which lights up behind and illuminates them. It is this little glow which makes for true beauty.' (PB. 142)

66. 'We stand bawling side by side without hearing or seeing each other and we say: what a desert is life! Happily there are still a few old ladies about who, for their part, have given up such nonsense and are beginning to see things clearly, at the age, alas, when they have to start wearing glasses.' (PB. 145)

'I find man too modest. He allows himself to be led even though it is almost always up to him to decide and though he is practically indomitable. Love, sickness, stupidity, he finds it convenient to lump them all under 'fatality'. But I recognize only death.' (PB. 40, 41)

'ISABELLE: Oh, monsieur Horace, it's wicked to think only of playing!
HORACE: My dear, we have just the time for that before being quite dead.' (PB. 102)

Chapter Five

68. 'What makes us shudder may also make us laugh.'
'nothing is so simple' (PG. 55)
69. 'There is love, of course. And then there is life, its enemy.' (PG. 14)
71. 'I can tell when the dog in the farmyard goes looking at night for the bitch in heat; I can tell when they take the bull to the village, and all the animals of the forest, under the earth, in the grass and in the trees . . . And the weasels and the badgers and the ferrets and the foxes in the clearing and the insects, the millions and millions of insects, in silence everywhere. They are all coupling, making love and killing me . . . All disgusting, you are all disgusting with your love.' (PG. 79)
'When he took me that first night, I thought I would die of contempt and loathing. But I loved. I moaned with joy beneath him . . . thinking only of my own pleasure, I forgot you until morning.' (PG. 77)
72. 'Come dance with your old skeleton, your old chronic disease. Come dance with your remorse. Come dance with your love.' (PG. 182)
73. 'One must never understand one's enemy – nor one's wife. In fact, one must never understand anyone, or the results can be fatal.' (PG. 208)
'derisory couple'
'overgrown little boy who does not ask for much' (PG. 210)
'I knew very well what I was doing when I cast this play.' (PB. 390)
75. 'a return to the old French source of Molière and the *fabliaux*.'
'a very ancient style of playing which goes back to the Atellan farces and which has been handed down through the *Commedia dell'Arte* and the trestle theatres of the Pont Neuf, to produce the *Illustre Théâtre* and, I am convinced, the acting style of the patron saint of French theatre.' (Molière)

76. 'vaudevillesque and caricatural process'
'Here at last is a dramatist who understands that the theatre is first and foremost a free game of the intellect and that verisimilitude, a carefully developed plot, cleverly arranged entrances and exists mean nothing.'
77. 'The play flows nonchalantly on and we are not terribly sure whence it comes or where it is going. So what? Leave the laws of architecture to building specialists. The theatre is a game of the intellect and the intellect can quite easily gather its honey by buzzing, like the bee, from detail to detail.'
'at one and the same time a marionnette and a human being.'
78. 'the even flatter image, if that is possible, of the already terribly conventional image which men create for themselves of their existence.'
'mankind's effort to render the reality around him sublime or reasonable.'
'we live in a farcical world and we dare not see that we do.'
'we are funny even when we think ourselves noble or touching'
'Consider this word 'the whole'. According to whether or not one takes account of the whole, one enters maturity or remains in childhood.'
79. 'a scenario by Max Sennet or Feydeau, conveying to us true, sometimes tragic, emotions which are rendered harmless and appropriate to a game of the intellect by a process of caricatural distortion. It is up to us to play with them. The game is not dangerous, it is essentially healthy in spirit and eminently moral in outcome . . . and we laugh throughout, even and especially at those moments when we ought to cry . . .'
'skirt the horrors of Strindberg'
80. 'the tiresome philosophers of despair who, periodically and somewhat ingenously, discover the horror of the human condition.'
81. 'properly speaking, the elegant and graceful story of a crime.' (PB. 375)
83. 'There is a simple, obvious fact that people forget: we belong to the same profession.'
'Molière, within a mould of intellectual comedy, has written the blackest theatre of any literature in any age.'
84. 'only ever intended to make people laugh'
'Molière the actor must have played like that. He too grimaced and gesticulated too much for the balcony, who turned up their noses while the stalls roared with laughter.''

Chapter Six

85. 'Even today, I think it is the kind of theatre I would have wanted to write. I believe I came close to it in *Ardèle* and *La Valse des Toréadors*.

The failure of *La Valse des Toréadors* was a fatal accident for me. Unconsciously, I switched tracks.'
'an inexplicable joy'
'she has all her life to act out first' (PC. 12)

86. 'Joan accepting everything, Joan getting fat, eating well . . . Can you see Joan in make-up, wearing a hat and hampered by layers of dresses, with a little dog – or a man – at her heels, who knows even, Joan married?' (PC. 131)
87. 'beginning a new life'
88. 'I did not consult books to find out what Henry II was really like – nor even Becket. I created the King I wanted and the ambiguous Becket I wanted.'
'to do well what I have to do' (PC. 196)
90. 'it is absolutely not a political play.'
91. 'For fifty years I have suffered. It is beginning to seem long. As a little boy, I had a vision of life which I have never got over.' (NPG. 38)
'Suddenly, one fine morning, by chance . . . I discovered the existence of the maggots. I was saved! . . . I noticed that if things were rotten in the state of France, it was because of the maggots in the apple. It all became clear at last: France was worm-eaten!' (NPG. 12, 13)
93. 'We dance the little ballet of desire like dogs. I sniff you, you sniff me, I turn away, I come back again, I don't want to, yes I do! And since I do, then it's for life. And then suddenly, someone (we don't know who) pulls on the lead and the little dog who was dreaming of eternity is whisked away . . .' (PG. 275)
94. 'One man in a thousand outgrows his childhood'
95. 'with a fearful curiosity' (PG. 440)
'But I love nobody. Not even the people. They stink like my father who used to beat me and like my mother's lovers who continued after his death. And I have a horror of everything that stinks.' (PG. 494)
96. 'The feeling of frightening you all is sweet too' (PG. 495)
'Poor Robespierre who kills because he has not managed to grow up.' (PG. 466)
'God is on the side of right and the English' (PC. 25)
'The ace is God, if you like, but in each camp.' (PC. 75)
97. 'We are powerless . . . we can do nothing but play our parts, each his own, good or bad, as it is written and when our turn comes.' (PC. 30)
'a story which ends well' (PC. 139)
'good old politics' (PC. 84)
'the excellence of her theological virtues'
'a saint who met her death in a political affair'
98. 'Me, I have slipped into the line by cheating – I am doubly illegitimate.' (PC. 187)
'the product of an era when human relations – based on the fidelity of one man to another – were simple.'
'improvise his honour' (PC. 187)
'My Prince . . . if you were my true prince, if you were of my race,

how simple everything would be. With what tenderness I would have surrounded you in an ordered world, my prince. Each man subject to another, from the lowest to the highest, bound by oath and never having to ask oneself anything ever again.' (PC. 187)
'He loves nothing on earth but the idea which he has forged of his honour.' (PC. 265)

99. 'The only thing which is immoral, my prince, is not doing what you must, when you must.' (PC. 208)
'England will owe him her final victory over disorder.' (PC. 295)
'It is an ugly sight, the spectacle of this giving of oneself. What obscene egoism.' (PG. 261)
'the terrible bitterness of those who have been right.'

100. 'Those poems are no longer by me. I detest hearing them mentioned. It's when I was living in an attic in the Latin Quarter with my head in the clouds, that I should have been congratulated about them.' (PG. 234)
'the tone has changed a lot since' (PG. 238)
'on the day of Judgement . . it will be seen that only those who have made men laugh will have performed a really useful service on this earth. I do not give much for the chances of the reformers, or the prophets, but there will always be a few frivolous individuals who will be revered forever. They alone will have helped men forget death.' (PG. 241)
'atomic bomb or not, we have always been temporary inhabitants of this planet. That has not prevented us from laughing from time to time.' (NPG. 87)

101. 'Hurry up, Toto, you are taking forever to grow up.' (NPG. 158)

Chapter Seven

102. 'Usually, it is in the plays one has been unable to write that one has the most to say'
'The dramatist is prisoner of the contingencies of both the theatre and society: his art is essentially social in character.'
'The play you are going to see this evening is one I have never been able to write.' (NPG. 165)

103. 'Your story was quite straightforward after all, you see. It's you who tended to complicate things.' (NPG. 292)

104. 'The theatre is a ball game in which more often than not, the ball lands on the audience's head. If the ball lands in a corner of the auditorium where there are clumsy people who cannot return it, then the game is spoiled; it is as simple as that. But *we* have been rehearsing for six weeks. *You* have not.' (NPG. 166)
'a very simple and very pure story' (NPG. 184)
'I cannot believe that life can be as ugly as that. There are good,

decent people everywhere, after all. We have a duty to say so and to write plays where there are decent people and fine sentiments . . . Who cares about literature! Only writers imagine it has any importance.' (NPG. 279)

105. 'laugh with him at all the sorrow and absurdity he could see in the human condition.'
'our Mother the Earth' (NPG. 183)
'an enormous figure, a female Falstaff, something Shakespearian' (NPG. 221)

106. 'Ah Adèle! She is my sorrow and my remorse. I carry on my shoulders the burden of shame for all that will happen to her. Perhaps I ought not to have spoken to her; perhaps I ought not to have made her understand certain things; that would have been easier for her.' (NPG. 196)
'You should not have invented me and given me the destiny and the mother you did. You should not have created my shame . . . For you, it was only a caprice of the imagination; you were doing your job, trying to write a play. Perhaps you should not have, but you have. So you must let us be now and not intervene again until the end.' (NPG. 261)
'There are already enough thorny issues in this damn play. Well! No! He's a Seminarian. You will just have to put up with him as I have had to.' (NPG. 169)

107. 'All the characters were important in this story. It is because of that I could not manage to write it. I would have needed a separate story, with all its ramifications, for each of them.' (NPG. 196)
'It was to bring her to life, to lift her out of the vague world of possibility and, with my meagre talent, give her some small measure of reality that I wanted to write this play.' (NPG. 183)
'You know well, you all have your roles.' (NPG. 185)
'I would have liked there to be no décor, nothing but characters in this play. But that proved impossible.' (NPG. 168)

108. 'an artificial character, the dregs of the old Boulevard theatre.' (NPG. 240)

109. 'I know perfectly well what I wanted to say in *La Grotte*. The fact that I have not managed to write the play does not mean I do not know.' (NPG. 240)
'which has nothing to do with the story and which I always put into my plays to help me to get things going' (NPG. 169)

110. 'Modern theatre has taken a great step forward. It has put an end to playing for play's sake and to entertaining.' (NPG. 87)

111. 'strangle the anecdote'
'I hear a critic whispering in his neighbour's ear that he has already seen this in Pirandello.' (NPG. 167)
'It is to be hoped that the public will applaud even so.' (NPG. 292)

Chapter Eight

112. 'We are all the omnipotent and, most of the time, ineffective, producers of an intimate opera: our lives.'
'a thousand reasons, both private and public.'
'a profound, emotional opposition'
'I was performed while he was in power. I stopped writing and I did not want to be performed in state theatres like the Comédie-Française. No, that I did not want.'
113. 'It hurts, believe me, to be slated as unmercifully as I have been.'
'You invite people to dinner and they repay you with gross ingratitude. One fine day you tell yourself that they are no longer worth cooking for. That is what I told myself.'
'I have certainly created an impact in the theatre but when that is repeated over twenty five years, it loses its force.'
'quite different'
114. 'Everyone lives in families, with wives and children . . . I have had a lot of children and they are very difficult to rear. Men fail with their children as they fail in their loves. It requires talent to be a lover, to be a father.'
115. 'This voracious family which I complain about, what exactly will I have given them when the final account is added up?' (PBQ. 313)
116. 'What about me? What about me? *I* exist too!' (PBQ. 55)
'I had this theatre . . . I have spent my whole life among these bits of scenery. My dances were those in my plays.' (PBQ. 159)
117. 'The light changes; during the fight, Alberto loses his moustache and his high collar. When everyone rushes in to separate them, it is Bachman with whom Julien is now fighting.' (PBQ. 221)
118. 'an illusion which deceives us on the spur of the moment' (NPG. 547)
'we always attach an exaggerated importance to the present' (PS. 156)
'since we persist stubbornly in splashing about in the current instead of watching the river flow by, we become victims of optical illusions' (PBQ. 174)
'It all happens at the same time. And it is always the same.' (PBQ. 22)
119. 'Life seems like a production at the Châtelet because there is always a big cast and lots of noise but, in the end, you perceive that there were really only four or five actors and that the play was hidden behind so many useless theatrical effects.' (PBQ. 47)
120. 'that theatrical instant when the truth of life will emerge.'
'the true text is the one which is never spoken' (PBQ. III)
'CRAVATAR: Well, that's done it, this time, we're trapped! Antoine will have pulled it off once again, his *fin d'acte*! The avalanche! (*He shouts on the verge of hysteria*) What bad taste! Ah, what abominable drama!
CARLOTTA: How admirable! Straight out of Sardou!' (PBQ. 40)
121. 'We will discover nothing. We never discover anything. We die without discovering anything.' (PBQ. 117)

'a pretext, somewhat outlandish in tone' (PBQ. 93)
'over the moment the curtain rises' (PBQ. 83)
'enormous error in casting' (PBQ. 117)

122. 'It was not you who were speaking, it was you *as seen by me*. There is no way out. We are trapped. All we know about other people is the image of them we create for ourselves.' (PBQ. 112)
'already someone else's predecessors' (PBQ. 236)
'Since the evolution of attitudes and the new generation . . . There's new muscle in the theatre, and new blood; look at Bataille and young Bernstein! Everything is on the move!' (PBQ. 25)
'this new pretension to writing scenes containing nothing but banalities' (PBQ. 83)
'the kind of Russian play they are trying to palm off on us at the moment' (PBQ. 83)

123. 'some theatrical device would have to be found to serve it up again' (PBQ. 133)

124. 'Life is a noisy, third-rate dance hall! And Greek tragedy, likewise!' (PS. 42)
'Her own mother has made Electre's heart into that of a ravaging wolf which will never be satiated.' (PS. 45)
'Only our professions are real and these, at least, we can try to make a success of.'

125. 'He has courage – which in the last analysis is the only virtue – he rebuilds the world every morning, ready to see it collapse again every evening, with a certain childlike naivety which is probably one of his charms . . . He thinks that we must always try something and that destiny, on the whole, is absent-minded.'
'The Avant-garde surely never changes. It never becomes classic. It remains what it is . . . To tell the truth, it is an attitude of mind, at least in my opinion. It seems to me that you do not need to be avant-garde minded in order to introduce a new note.'

126. 'the secret influence is felt everywhere'
'played almost entirely in long-johns and night-shirts, like a Feydeau farce.'
'we will laugh often'

127. 'Popescu uses the absurd to make people laugh. Your kind of comedy is outdated. We don't feel involved anymore. You couldn't bring yourself to feel a little of the tragedy and absurdity of the human condition, could you? That would be asking too much of you, wouldn't it? A man with any heart would do it – at least for his family! But no, not you! You make it a point of honour to be out of date.' (NPG. 463)
'that very old habit of talking lightly – and thinking lightly – about everything.' (NPG. 579)

Conclusion

128. 'I am a workman of the theatre. I take a delight in the craftsman side of things.'

129. 'My father was a tailor's cutter. He was a sensitive and simple man with a marvellous knowledge of his craft. He knew both the standards it imposed and the pride it gave him. "Going to the bad" in literature, I have always dreamed of being as fine a craftsman as he. Even my critics admit that I have succeeded in this. I am, therefore, a good maker of plays. Without false modesty, I have, as the saying goes, a trade at my fingertips.'

 'My father loved his craft which is an art. From him, I really understood the meaning of professional conscientiousness and the nobility it confers on a man.'

 'We all have one or two problems which interest us particularly and which we come back to . . . In the end, the plays develop a family likeness.'

130. 'I get the impression that all my early plays have been written by my father . . . It is true that Antigone irritates me. Her tribulations would be unbearable were it not for the fact she is a child.'

132. 'I think that was my first revelation in the theatre. The basic ingredients of my work are to be found there: comedy, conventionality, melodrama, the love interest. I have remained with the theatre of my childhood.'

 'to such an extent that I see people lying: I can no longer go to a funeral without saying to myself, in the midst of all the lamentations, "that lady is lying, my goodness what a bad liar she is." '

 'this fascinating and corrupt world of the theatre before the First World War'

133. 'Man can only know true reality, which is formless, by giving it a form. The art of the theatre is to give it as artificial and arbitrary a form as possible and, by that means, to be more real than reality.'

 'a pretext, somewhat outlandish in tone' (PBQ. 93)

134. 'Moreover, there are underground trains at rush hour and ticket queues in stations where people perform very good avant-garde theatre, without realizing it.'

 'it is still there, as permanent as a sentry at his post, identical in every detail to what it was in 1920.'

 'Inspiration is only a series of variations on eternal themes.'

135. 'Some of us in the business have been trying since the Great War to strangle plot and kill the notion of the 'well-made play' which has dominated the French stage since Scribe. We want to embalm and bury it. Pirandello, in a stroke of genius the importance of which can never be exaggerated, took the trouble to strangle it to death one day with his 'Six Characters in Search of an Author".

 'Some people say I am out-of-date, no longer with it. They would like me to write serious plays and discuss philosophical principles. But I

can't take myself seriously enough.'
'There is one misunderstanding above all which I fear. You know my theme? I only hope people are not going to interpret it in terms of a class struggle.'

136. 'profound, emotional opposition'
'I have no political thoughts. My dislikes are instinctive.'
'I am not interested in social criticism. It is enough to ridicule man.'
'for a long time to come, hatred belongs to the French' (PG. 418)
'infantile, like we are all in the process of becoming'
'We must accept being governed . . . Attaching too much importance to the money taken from you or the actions demanded of you, in the street, by the police, is the most futile and unconsidered attitude imaginable. But to allow yourself to be led by destiny . . . that is unforgiveable.' (PB. 40, 41)

137. 'Thanks to Molière, the real French theatre is the only one where, instead of saying masses, we laugh, like men at war . . . at all the misery and horror of our existence.'
'discover, periodically and somewhat ingenuously, the horror of the human condition and who would like to prevent us amusing ourselves in the theatre.'

138. 'The spread of culture will certainly multiply, in the years to come, the already considerable number of those who labour by the intellect . . . the number of comic authors will not change.'
'We come to the theatre to take part in a game of the intellect (which does not at all mean playing intellectual games)'
'The explosive force of one phrase has produced the same effect as an entire chapter of Montaigne; in less than a second, in a flash, we have learned the truth – the whole truth – about man and we have laughed. But neither Molière, who did not know a second before that he was going to write this phrase, nor we, have *thought* during this very brief and violent phenomenon.'
'I am aiming neither at posterity nor the respect of my contemporaries.'

Appendix II

There follows a chronology of Anouilh's creative and professional life, listing the plays, adaptations, films or other works in which Anouilh was engaged in successive years. A = adaptation, B = book, story, etc., C = cinema film. Bracketed plays remain unfinished, unpublished, and/or unproduced.

1929 *Humulus le Muet*
(Mandarine)
1930 *(Attila le Magnifique)*
1931 *L'Hermine*
1932 *Jézabel*
Le Bal des Voleurs
1934 *La Sauvage*
Y avait un prisonnier
1935 *(Le Petit Bonheur)*
1936 *Le Voyageur sans bagage*
Les Dégourdis de la onzième (C)
1937 *Le Rendez-vous de Senlis*
Vous n'avez rien à déclarer (C)
1938 *(L'Incertain)*[1]
1939 *Léocadia*
Les Otages (C)
L'Histoire de Monsieur Mauvette et de la fin du monde (B pub.)
Cavalcade d'amour (C)
1940 *Marie-Jeanne ou la fille du peuple* (A)
1941 *Eurydice*
1942 *Antigone*
(Oreste)
1943 *Le Voyageur sans bagage* (C)
1945 *Roméo et Jeannette*
1946 *Médée*
L'Invitation au château

[1] Listed in Kelly, *Annotated Bibliography*, p. 88.

1947 *Monsieur Vincent* (C)
Anna Karénine (C)
1948 *Ardèle ou la Marguerite*
Épisode de la vie d'un auteur
Pattes blanches (C)
Les Demoiselles de la Nuit (Ballet scenario)
1949 *Cécile ou l'école des pères*
1950 *La Répétition ou l'amour puni*
Colombe
Caroline chérie (C)
1951 *La Valse des Toréadors*
Deux sous de violettes (C)
1952 *L'Alouette*
Le Rideau rouge (C)
Un Caprice de Caroline chérie (C)
Trois Comédies de Shakespeare (B pub.)
1953 *Désir sous les ormes* (A)
Le Chevalier de la nuit (C)
Le Loup (Ballet scenario)
1954 *Il est important d'être aimé* (A)
1955 *Ornifle ou le courant d'air*
1956 *Pauvre Bitos ou le dîner de têtes*
L'Hurluberlu ou le réactionnaire amoureux
1957 *L'Orchestre*
1958 *Becket ou l'honneur de Dieu*
La Foire d'empoigne
1959 *La Petite Molière*
Madame de . . . (A)
1960 *La Grotte*
Le Songe du critique
Tartuffe (A)
1961 *Fables* (B)
La Nuit des rois (A)
La Mort de Belle (C)
Colombe (Opera libretto)
1962 *Victor ou les enfants au pouvoir* (A)
L'Amant complaisant (A)
1963 *L'Acheteuse* (A)
La Ronde (C)
1964 *Ne réveillez pas Madame*
Richard III (A)
1966 *Le Boulanger, la boulangère et le petit mitron*
L'Ordalie ou la Petite Catherine de Heilbronn (A)

1967 *Cher Antoine ou l'amour raté*
Monsieur Barnett
(La belle vie)[1]
1968 *Les Poissons rouges ou mon père ce héros*
Chansons bêtes[2]
1969 *Tu étais si gentil quand tu étais petit*
1970 *Le Directeur de l'Opéra*
Madame de . . . (Opera libretto)
1971 *L'Arrestation*
1974 *Le Scénario*
1976 *Chers Zoiseaux*
Le jeune homme et le lion (Television play)
1978 *La Culotte*

[1] Listed in Marsh, p. 201.
[2] Musical entertainment based on the *Fables*.

Bibliography

Works of Anouilh

The Plays

Anouilh's collected plays are published by La Table Ronde under the following titles, which are given in chronological order, the dates being of recent reprints:

Pièces roses (1973), *Pièces noires* (1970), *Nouvelles pièces noires* (1970), *Pièces brillantes* (1972), *Pièces grinçantes* (1973), *Nouvelles pièces grinçantes* (1970), *Pièces costumées* (1967), *Pièces baroques* (1974), *Pièces secrètes* (1977).

A number of critical editions of individual plays are also available:

La Répétition, ed. G. Lerminier, Classiques Larousse, 1957.
Antigone, ed. W. M. Landers, Harrap, 1960.
Le Bal des Voleurs, ed. W. D. Howarth, Harrap, 1960.
Léocadia, with *Humulus le Muet*, ed. B. Fielding, Harrap, 1961.
Pauvre Bitos, ed. W. D. Howarth, Harrap, 1961.
L'Alouette, ed. Thomas and Lee, Methuen, 1964.
Antigone, ed. R. Laubreaux, Didier, 1964.
Becket, ed. W. D. Howarth, Harrap, 1964.
Antigone, ed. J. Monférier, Bordas, 1968.
Eurydice, ed. G. Rambert, Bordas, 1968.
Le Valse des Toréadors, ed. C. King, Harrap, 1968.
La Répétition, ed. Ph. Sellier, Bordas, 1970.

Other works by Anouilh

Y avait un prisonnier, play not included in the collected works; *La Petite Illustration*, no. 370, May 18th 1935.

Épisode de la vie d'un auteur, curtain-raiser performed with *Ardèle; Cahiers de la Compagnie Renaud-Barrault*, vol. 26, May 1959.

La Petite Molière, originally a film script written in collaboration with R. Laudenbach, adapted for the stage; *L'Avant-Scène*, Dec. 15th 1959.

Le Songe du critique, curtain-raiser performed with Anouilh's production of *Tartuffe; L'Avant-Scène*, May 15th 1961.

Monsieur Barnett, one-act play; *L'Avant-Scène*, March 1st 1975.

Il est important d'être aimé, translated and adapted from Oscar Wilde, *The Importance of Being Earnest; L'Avant-Scène*, no. 101, 1955.

La Nuit des Rois, translated and adapted from Shakespeare, *Twelfth Night*; *L'Avant-Scène*, May 15th 1961.

Tartuffe, adapted from Molière; *L'Avant-Scène*, May 15th 1961.

Victor ou les enfants au pouvoir, adapted from Roger Vitrac; *L'Avant-Scène*, Nov. 15th 1962.

L'Amant complaisant, translated and adapted from Graham Greene, *The Complacent Lover*; Paris, Robert Laffont, 1962.

L'Ordalie ou la Petite Catherine de Heilbronn, translated and adapted from Kleist, *Das Kätchen von Heilbronn; L'Avant-Scène*, no. 372, 1967.

L'Histoire de Monsieur Mauvette et de la fin du monde, short story; *Cahiers de la Compagnie Renaud-Barrault*, vol. 26, May 1959.

Fables, a collection of verse fables for our time; Paris, La Table Ronde, 1962.

Trois Comédies de Shakespeare (*Comme il vous plaira, Un conte d'hiver, La Nuit des Rois*) in collaboration with Claude Vincent; La Table Ronde, 1952.

Articles and Interviews

1. 'Le rôle du théâtre n'est pas de faire vrai', interview with Yvon Novy; *Jour*, March 12th 1935.
2. 'Un nouveau venu, Monsieur Jean Anouilh, âgé de 24 ans dont la troisième pièce sera jouée aux Ambassadeurs', interview with Gabriel Reuillard; *Excelsior*, March 17th 1935.
3. 'Jean Anouilh et l'artifice', reported interview; *Les Nouvelles Littéraires*, March 27th 1937.
4. 'Rencontre avec Jean Anouilh pendant la générale de *La Sauvage*, interview with André Warnod; *Le Figaro*, Jan. 11th 1938.
5. Reported interview with Yvon Novy; *Comœdia*, Nov. 15th 1941.
6. Interview with Eugène Borel; *Gavroche*, Nov. 5th 1947.
7. 'Des ciseaux de papa au sabre de mon père'; *Opéra*, March 7th 1951.
8. 'Ludmilla Pitöeff'; *Opéra*, Sept. 19th 1951.
9. 'La farce de mœurs est née'; *Paris-Presse*, Oct. 14th 1951.
10. Interview with André Thierry; *Arts*, Nov. 16th 1951.
11. 'Le Secret de Jean Anouilh', interview with Francis Ambrière; *Les Annales*, XV, Jan. 1952.
12. '*La Valse des Toréadors*? Que voilà une bonne piece!'; *Le Figaro*, Jan. 23rd 1952.
13. 'Jean Anouilh, muet par principe, se cache derrière son *Rideau rouge*', interview; *L'Aurore*, Nov. 15th 1952.
14. 'Godot ou le sketch des pensées de Pascal traité par les Fratellini'; *Arts*, Feb. 27th 1953.

15. 'Anouilh returns', interview with Isolde Farrell; *New York Times*, Jan. 3rd 1954.
16. Preface to *Cécile ou l'école des pères; L'Avant-Scène*, no. 101, 1955.
17. 'La Mort d'une troupe'; *Arts*, Oct. 19th 1955.
18. 'Lettre d'un vieux crocodile à un jeune mousquetaire'; *Arts*, May 1st 1957.
19. 'Pour la première fois Anouilh parle . . .', interview with Jean Delavèze; *Les Nouvelles Littéraires*, Feb. 5th 1959.
20. 'Le théâtre d'aujourd'hui: Jean Anouilh', interview with André Frank; *Cahiers Renaud–Barrault*, vol. 26, May 1959. (Reprinted from *Les Nouvelles Littéraires*, Jan. 10th 1946.)
21. 'Ce soir-là à Bordeaux, Jean Anouilh ressuscitait Molière', interview; *Paris-Match*, June 13th 1959.
22. 'Ai-je du crédit?'; *Arts*, Oct. 14th 1959.
23. 'Il y a dix ans mourait Charles Dullin'; *Le Figaro*, Dec. 12th 1959.
24. 'Le bon Pain'; *Le Figaro*, June 9th 1960.
25. 'Becket by Chance'; *New York Times*, Oct. 2nd 1960.
26. 'Devant Shakespeare, je me sens encore comme un apprenti étonné; *Carrefour*, March 1st 1961.
27. 'Recontre avec Jean Anouilh', interview with Jean Nicollier; *La Gazette de Lausanne*, March 4th, 5th 1961.
28. Preface to *La Nuit des Rois; L'Avant-Scène*, May 15th 1961.
29. 'En présentant *Victor* de Roger Vitrac, j'essaie de réparer une injustice', interview with Claude Sarraute; *Le Monde*, Oct. 4th 1962.
30. 'Pour une fois Jean Anouilh s'est laissé interviewer', with Guy Verdot; *Le Figaro Littéraire*, Oct. 6th 1962.
31. 'Dans mon trou de souffleur pour la première fois au théâtre j'ai eu peur'; *Paris-Match*, Oct. 20th 1962.
32. 'Un rôle inattendu pour Jean Anouilh: le pélican', interview with Huguette Debaisieux; *Le Figaro*, Dec. 31st 1963.
33. 'A Walk and a Talk with Jean Anouilh', interview with J. Barry; *New York Times*, Sept. 13th 1964.
34. 'Non, Richard III n'est pas un mélo mouvementé, c'est un chef-d'œuvre plein de poésie', interview with Steve Passeur; *L'Aurore*, Nov. 14th, 15th 1964.
35. 'Pour un instant de théâtre; *Le Figaro*, Sept. 29th 1966.
36. 'Anouilh: je redécouvre *Becket*', interview with Pierre Montaigne; *Le Figaro* Oct. 26th 1966.
37. 'Entretien avec Jean Anouilh à propos de *Becket* et de l'échec de *La petite Catherine*', with Claude Sarraute; *Le Monde*, Nov. 1st 1966.
38. 'Jean Anouilh à Villars; Les Vaudois, je les connais trop!', interview with Valérie, *Tribune de Genève*, Dec. 22nd 1966.
39. Preface to *L'Ordalie ou la petite Catherine de Heilbronn, L'Avant-Scène*, no. 372, 1967.
40. 'De la culture et du bouillon'; *Le Figaro*, March 30th 1967.

41. 'Paris et Jean Anouilh ne s'entendent plus', interview with Michèle Motte; *L'Express*, Oct. 9th 1967.
42. 'Le Mystère Labiche', preface to vol. 5, *Œuvres complètes de Labiche* Paris, Club de l'honnête homme, 1968.
43. 'La Grâce; *Le Figaro*, Feb. 7th 1968.
44. Interview with D. M.; *L'Aurore*, May 2nd 1968.
45. 'Anouilh prépare sa rentrée parisienne', interview with Edgar Schneider; *Paris-Presse*, July 27th 1968.
46. 'Mon grand virage', *Les Nouvelles Littéraires*, Nov. 14th 1968.
47. 'Jean Anouilh: je souris . . . donc j'ai changé', interview; *Paris-Jour*, Sept. 8th 1969.
48. 'La Volonté générale'; *Le Figaro*, June 5th 1970.
49. 'I write plays as a chair-maker makes chairs', interview with T. Q. Curtiss; *International Herald-Tribune*, Sept. 18th 1970.
50. 'Avertissement prudent', preface to *Tu étais si gentil . . .*; *L'Avant-Scène*, July 15th 1972.
51. 'Je n'ai rencontré qu'un génie dans ma vie: Pitoëff', interview with Nicolas de Rabaudy; *Paris-Match*, Oct. 21st 1972.
52. 'Les Sources'; *Le Figaro*, Nov. 29th 1972.
53. 'Un affreux cas de népotisme'; *L'Avant-Scène*, May 1st 1974.
54. 'Faire rire', preface to revival of *La Valse des Toréadors; L'Avant-Scène*, May 15th 1974.
55. Preface to *La Traversée d'une vie* by Françoise Rosay; Paris, Robert Laffont, 1974.
56. 'Jean Anouilh, playwright in retreat', interview with Glenys Roberts; *Radio Times*, July 9th–15th 1977.

General Works

ARCHER, Marguerite, *Jean Anouilh*; New York, Columbia U.P., 1971.

BARSACQ, André and TOUCHARD, Pierre-Aimé, *Roméo et Jeannette; Le Spectateur*, Feb. 11th 1947.

BORGAL, Clément, *Anouilh: la peine de vivre*; Paris, Éditions du Centurion, 1966.

BRUSTEIN, Robert, *The Theatre of Revolt*; London, Methuen, 1965.

CAMUS, Albert, *Le Mythe de Sisyphe*; Paris, Gallimard, 1974.

DELLA FAZIA, Alba, *Jean Anouilh*; New York, Twayne, 1969.

DIDIER, Jean, *A la Rencontre de Jean Anouilh*; Brussels, La Sixaine, 1946.

FRANK, André, *Théâtre vieilli et théâtre neuf: Jean Anouilh à la croisée des chemins*; *La Gazette des Lettres*, April 27th 1946.

FRYE, Northrop, *Anatomy of Criticism*; New Jersey, Princeton U.P., 1957.

GHÉON, Henri, *L'Art du théâtre*; Montréal, Serge, 1944.

GIGNOUX, Hubert, *Jean Anouilh*; Paris, Temps Présent, 1946.

GINESTIER, Paul, *Jean Anouilh*; Paris, Seghers, 1969.

GROSSVOGEL, David, *The Self-conscious Stage in Modern French Drama*; New York, Columbia U.P., 1958.

HARVEY, John, *Anouilh: a Study in Theatrics*; New Haven, Yale U.P., 1964.

HOWARTH, W. D. and THOMAS, M. (ed.), *Molière: Stage and Study. Essays in honour of W. G. Moore*; Oxford, Clarendon Press, 1973.

JOHN, S., 'Obsession and Techniques in the Plays of Jean Anouilh'; *French Studies*, vol. XI, April 1957.

JOLIVET, Philippe, *Le Théâtre de Jean Anouilh*; Paris, Michel Brient, 1963.

KELLY, Kathleen W., *Jean Anouilh: an Annotated Bibliography*; New Jersey, Scarecrow Press, 1973.

KITTO, H. D. F., *Form and Meaning in Drama*; London, Methuen, 1968.

KNOWLES, Dorothy, *French Drama of the Inter-War Years*; London, Harrap, 1967.

LASALLE, Jean-Pierre, *Jean Anouilh ou la vaine révolte*; Rodez, Subervie, 1958.

LUCAS, F. L., *Tragedy: Serious Drama in Relation to Aristotle's Poetics*; London, Hogarth Press, 1966.

LUPPE, Robert de, *Jean Anouilh*; Paris, Éditions Universitaires, 1959.

MALACHY, Thérèse, *Jean Anouilh: les problèmes de l'existence dans un théâtre de marionnettes*; Paris, Nizet, 1978.

MARCEL, Gabriel, *L'Heure théâtrale*; Paris, Plon, 1959.

MARCEL, Gabriel, *Roméo et Jeannette*; *Les Nouvelles Littéraires*, Dec. 12th 1946.

MARCEL, Gabriel, *De Jézabel à Médée: le tragique chez Jean Anouilh; Revue de Paris*, June 1949.

MARSH, Edward O., *Jean Anouilh: Poet of Pierrot and Pantaloon*; London, W. H. Allen, 1953.

MAZON, Paul, *Eschyle: Œuvres*, vol. 2; Paris, Les Belles-Lettres, 1961.

MURY, Gilbert, *Les Intellectuels devant l'action*; Paris, Seghers, 1946.

PRONKO, Leonard, C., *The World of Jean Anouilh*; Berkeley, California U.P., 1961.

RADINE, Serge, *Anouilh, Lenormand, Salacrou: trois dramaturges à la recherche de leur vérité*; Genève, Trois Collines, 1951.

RENAUD, M. and BARRAULT, J. L., *Cahiers de la Compagnie Renaud–Barrault*, vol. 26, May 1959.

ROMBOUT, André F., *La Pureté dans le théâtre de Jean Anouilh: amour et bonheur ou l'anarchisme réactionnaire*; Amsterdam, Holland Universiteits Pers, 1975.

SIMON, Pierre-Henri, *Théâtre et Destin: la signification de la renaissance dramatique en France au vingtième siècle*; Paris, Armand Colin, 1959.

STEINBERG, R. and MOWSHOWITZ, H., *La Répétition par Jean Anouilh: une nouvelle lecture*; Études françaises, vol. 9, no. 2, 1973.

SWERLING, Anthony, *Strindberg's Impact in France: 1920–1960*; Cambridge, Trinity Lane Press, 1971.

THODY, Philip, *Anouilh*; Edinburgh, Oliver and Boyd, 1968.

VANDROMME, Paul, *Jean Anouilh: un auteur et ses personnages*; Paris, La Table Ronde, 1965.

VIER Jacques, *Le Théâtre de Jean Anouilh*; Paris, S.E.D.E.S., 1976.

WALTER, Jean, *Pièces noires*; *Plaisir*, Dec. 12th 1945.

Index

Aeschylus, 123
Alceste, 92
L'Alouette, 85–87, 88, 90, 93, 94, 96–98, 99, 100, 101, 125, 133
Anouilh
  anti-intellectualism, 8, 78–79, 83–84, 100–101, 137–138
  craftsmanship, 7, 8, 9, 19, 65, 128–129, 137
  and his critics, 76, 85, 89, 112–113, 128, 129
  early thirties, 23, 28–29
  as entertainer, 8–9, 11, 104–105, 137
  ethics, 11, 39, 41, 43–45, 54, 66, 83, 129, 136
  evolution, 14–15, 19, 23, 28, 43, 59, 65, 67, 68, 74–75, 83, 112
  father, 128, 129
  fear of ridicule, 59, 65
  grandfather, 128, 129
  inspiration, 64–65, 104–106, 129–130, 134
  marriages, 59, 87
  modesty, 11, 128, 138–139
  mother, 128, 131
  naturalism,14–15, 22, 23, 24, 32, 35, 39, 86
  poverty, 19–20, 28
  privacy, 11
  war years, 42–43, 59–60, 136
Anouilh, Catherine, 28
Anouilh, Nicole, 87
Antigone, 8, 44–45, 48, 49–50, 51–55, 65, 80, 83, 86, 93, 130, 131, 133
Arcachon, 131–132
Ardèle, 68, 69, 70–72, 75, 76, 77, 85, 114, 131
L'Arrestation, 118–119, 125, 131
Atelier, Théâtre de l', 27
Atellan Farces, 75, 84, 137
Augier, Émile, 138, 139
Avant-garde, The, 8, 92, 110–111, 122, 123, 125, 134–135

Bal des Voleurs, Le, 14, 20, 24–27, 28, 30, 32, 33, 35, 39, 60, 61, 63
Bataille, Henri, 122
Becket, 60, 87–89, 93, 94, 96, 98–99, 125, 133
Becket, Thomas à, 8, 87–89
Beckett, Samuel, 8, 110, 134, 135
Bernstein, Henri, 122
Birth of Tragedy, The, 42
Bordeaux, 129, 131
Boulanger, Le, 112, 113, 116, 118, 125, 126
Boulevard comedy, 14, 24
  theatre, 120
Brasillach, Robert, 59–60, 112, 136

Camus, Albert, 42, 99, 135
Caricature, 22, 38–39, 55, 70, 73, 76, 77–79, 86, 91, 92, 97
Chaises, Les, 110
Chaplin, Charlie, 75
Characterization, 22–23, 34–35, 38–39, 44–45, 46, 49, 50, 77–78, 86, 88, 92, 106–108, 132
Chekhov, Anton, 122
Cher Antoine, 111, 119–123, 125, 128, 134
Cherry Orchard, The, 122
Chers Zoiseaux, 114, 115, 131
Childhood, 10, 21, 46, 48, 58, 71, 78–79, 96, 99, 101, 116–117, 124, 131
Choephori, The, 123
Cinema, 7, 29, 75, 87, 92, 128
Circus, 75
Cocteau, Jean, 42, 51
Collaboration, 60, 88, 89, 93, 97, 98
Colombe, 55, 68, 69–70, 74, 77, 130
Comédie des Champs-Élysées, La 110
Comédie-Française, La, 112
Commedia dell'Arte, 75, 130
Compromise, 10, 42, 43, 48, 53, 54, 55, 58, 68, 69, 94
Culotte, La, 114, 115

Danse macabre, 74
Death, 42, 51, 54, 56, 66, 83, 93, 137

De Gaulle, 60, 112, 136
Directeur de l'Opéra, Le, 114, 115, 124–125
Don Juan, 90, 99
Double Inconstance, La, 73, 80–82
Drame, 51, 52, 54, 75
Dumas fils, Alexandre, 138, 139

L'École des Femmes, 74
Eliot, T. S., 85
L'Épuration, 59, 89, 93, 112, 118
Euripides, 47
Eurydice, 42, 45–46, 47, 55, 93
Existentialism, 8

Fables, 128
Fabliaux, Les, 75
Family, 10, 18, 21, 30, 31, 32, 92, 114–115, 116, 117, 119, 123–124, 130
Farce, 68, 70, 71, 72, 73, 74, 75, 76, 91
Feydeau, Georges, 79, 126
French Revolution, The, 89, 116
Freud, Sigmund, 94, 115, 126

Genet, Jean, 135
Ghelderode, Michel de, 68
Gilbert and Sullivan, 132
Giraudoux, Jean, 42, 75
Grotte, La, 87, 102–111, 112, 113, 114, 122, 125,
Guignol, Le, 75

Hamlet, 124
Happiness, 17, 19, 36, 46, 50, 86, 130
Henry II, 88
L'Hermine, 15–16, 17–18, 20, 28, 33, 132
Histoire de la conquête de l'Angleterre par les Normands, 88
Histoire de Monsieur Mauvette et de la fin du monde, 128
Hop Signor! 68
Humulus le muet, 14
L'Hurluberlu, 91–92, 94, 100, 101, 110, 114, 130, 131, 134

Idealism, 10, 42, 43, 45, 51, 54–55, 57, 58, 60, 68, 70, 74, 89, 91, 92, 94, 95–96, 99, 117, 130
L'Illustre Théâtre, 75
L'Invitation au château, 60–67, 74, 83, 87, 104, 131, 136–137
Ionesco, Eugène, 8, 110, 134, 135

Jézabel, 15, 16, 17, 18, 19, 20, 24, 28, 33, 114, 132
Joan of Arc, 8, 85, 97–98, 100–101
Jouvet, Louis, 28
Justice, 59, 89, 93, 94, 112, 135–136

Labiche, Eugène, 138
La Fontaine, Jean de, 128
Lançon, Nicole, 87
Laudenbach, Roland, 74
Léocadia, 31–32, 35, 39–41, 60, 61, 65
Liberation, The, 59–60, 88, 93, 112
Life
  absurdity of, 8, 25–26, 53, 58, 66, 79–80, 83, 100, 127, 133, 137
  as farce, 70, 74, 78, 119
  as game, 26, 63, 90, 130
  melodrama of, 33–34, 55–56
  as theatrical, 12, 20–21, 43, 119–121, 132, 133–134
  tragedy of, 51, 54, 100, 119, 137
Linder, Max, 75
Louis XVI, 95, 116
Love, 16, 27, 31, 32, 43, 45, 47, 52, 56, 59, 64, 68, 69, 70, 71, 72, 81–82, 88–89, 93, 116, 130
Ludic Approach, 29–30, 32–33, 38, 40, 43, 44, 79

Machine Infernale, La, 51, 52
Malade Imaginaire, Le, 91
Marie-Antoinette, 116
Marivaux, 73, 74, 75, 82
Mauriac, François, 60
Médée, 46–47, 56–57
Melodrama, 10, 14, 17, 33–34, 35, 47, 55–56, 64, 75, 76
Métier, 41, 53–54, 55, 58, 66, 67, 83, 116, 124, 129
Misanthrope, Le, 74, 92
Molière, 74, 75, 83–84, 90, 92, 133, 137, 138
Money, 15, 19, 61–62
Montaigne, 138
Montfort-l'Amaury, 87
Murder in the Cathedral, 85
Mythology, 42–58, 59, 75, 80, 123–124

Naturalistic drama, 26, 44, 45
Ne réveillez pas Madame, 113, 117–118, 119, 122, 124, 125, 128
Nietzsche, 37

Occupation, The, 8, 42, 60, 88
Old Testament, The, 96
Operetta, 64, 132
Ornifle, 90–91, 94, 99–100, 110, 113

Pantomine, 76, 90
Pascal, 59
Past, 10, 21, 30, 32, 36, 37, 43, 55, 95,

117–118, 119
Pauvre Bitos, 60, 89–90, 93, 94–96, 133, 135, 136
Pensées, Les, 59
Pirandello, Luigi, 24, 106, 110, 111, 134, 135
Pitoëff, Georges, 19, 39, 110
    Ludmilla, 19
Poissons rouges, Les, 60, 114, 118, 125, 127, 135
Politics, 50, 52, 53, 59–60, 63, 89–90, 93, 97–98, 99, 135–137
Predestination, 12, 27, 43, 48, 50, 51, 52, 55, 62, 63, 65, 66, 83, 97, 133
Purity, 10, 18, 21, 36, 71–72, 85

Realism, 41, 78
Rendez-vous de Senlis, Le, 31, 32, 34, 38–39, 43, 61, 74, 77
Répétition, La, 68, 73–74, 76, 77, 80–82, 84, 85
Resistance, The, 42, 88, 93
Revolt, 10, 17, 19, 21–22, 46, 50, 86, 117
Robespierre, 89, 94, 95, 96
Roméo et Jeannette, 43, 47, 48, 55–56, 57, 59

Sainval, Claude, 75
Sardou, Victorien, 120
Sartre, Jean-Paul, 8, 42, 135
Sauvage, La, 8, 16–23, 28, 29, 32, 33, 34, 61–62, 93, 114, 132, 135
Scénario, Le, 114
Scribe, Eugène, 120, 135
Seneca, 47
Sennet, Max, 75, 79
Sexuality, 69, 71–72, 131
Sganarelle, 91
Shakespeare, 47, 123, 124, 133
Siegfried, 42, 75
Six Characters in Search of an Author, 24, 110, 135
Sophocles, 46, 52, 53, 54
Strindberg, August, 74, 75, 79
Studio des Champs-Élysées, Le, 110
Surrealism, 75, 125–126

Taine, Hippolyte, 78
Television, 7, 128
Theatre
    function of, 10–11, 39, 58, 65–67, 82–84, 100, 110, 132, 133–134, 136–137
    as game, 26–27, 29–30, 32, 35–36, 37, 41, 44, 61, 66, 76, 79, 82, 83, 104, 109, 110, 133, 138
Theatricalism, 22–23, 35, 41, 43, 132–133, 135, 136
Thierry, Augustin, 88
Time, 117–119, 126
Tragedy, 10, 35, 48, 49, 51–54, 87, 123–124, 126, 133
Tu étais si gentil, 123–124, 126, 135

Valentin, Monelle, 20, 59
Valse des Toréadors, La, 68, 70, 72–73, 74, 75, 77, 79, 80, 84, 85, 87, 92, 105, 131
Vaudeville, 75, 76, 77, 78, 90, 126
Victor ou les enfants au pouvoir, 75, 126
Vitrac, Roger, 75, 77, 85, 126, 134
Voyageur sans bagage, Le, 8, 23, 24, 28, 29, 30–31, 32, 33–35, 36–38, 43, 55, 65, 76, 79, 131

Waiting for Godot, 110
Women's Liberation, 115

Y avait un prisonnier, 29